LONELY PLANET'S
ULTIMATE
TRAVEL
QUIZ
BOOK

CONTENTS

Chapter 3: Explorer (Hard)   111

INTRODUCTION

BY JOE FULLMAN

Welcome to the big, wide world of quizzing. This book is billed as a 'travel' quiz, but really it's an 'everything' quiz. After all, travel is about experiencing all the world has to offer, so we've tried to cram as much of the planet into these pages as we can. You'll be tested on everything from capitals to currencies, tallest buildings to longest rivers, national dishes to international airports, ancient empires to modern art galleries, the deepest lakes to the biggest oceans, and even outer space – perhaps the greatest travel adventure of all.

How it Works

There are 100 quizzes in all, most of which have 20 questions (some a little over, some a little under), amounting to a grand total of just over 2000 (2017 to be precise, which is always a valuable trait for quizzes). The majority are general knowledge, covering a wide selection of topics and regions – the whole planet is represented. We've also included a few themed rounds to test your expertise of a particular subject, including books, museums, film locations, landmarks, sports venues, wildlife and more.

Most questions require just a single answer, but there are a few multi-parters here and there, often the final question in a round. Some are multiple choice, so you can at least have a go even if you haven't got a clue. Be sure to read the options carefully – there's usually one that couldn't possibly be right, improving your chances to a 50-50 shot.

But a quick word of warning before you get too confident: things get more testing as you go on. The book is split into three chapters:

Day-Tripper: A gentle introduction to the world of travel quizzing – expect to get 15–20 of these ones right.

Traveller: A bit more challenging – your average will probably be lowered to around the 10–15 mark.

Explorer: Taking it up another notch, these questions are occasionally downright fiendish. If you get half of these right, you're doing pretty well.

Of course, the more help you get, the better you're likely to do. That's one of the great things about quizzing; it can be enjoyed both as a solo activity – methodically working your way through the questions – and with friends and family. And there really is no sense of satisfaction quite as smug as besting your loved ones in a quiz.

But there's no need to despair if you don't know an answer. Quizzing isn't just about recalling knowledge, it's about learning new stuff. The phrase 'Oh, I didn't know that' shouldn't be an admission of defeat so much as a statement of conquest because now you do, allowing you to squirrel that fact away for next time. It helps that there are some wonderful stories behind many of the answers (which is why they occasionally take the form of mini essays), such as why Vegemite changed its name to... well you'll find out in Quiz 78 if you don't know already, or why a bikini is called a bikini (Quiz 36) or what world-famous landmark the notorious conman Victor Lustig managed to sell to unsuspecting buyers, twice (Quiz 56).

A good question is often a prompt for further discussion and enquiry, sending you off on little research trips, diving down Wikipedia wormholes, helping you to hone and improve your quizzing game.

These days quizzing is a truly global phenomenon. The pub quiz, once a peculiarly British endeavour, in which groups of friends gather once a week to pool their collective wisdom in return for a meagre (or more often no) prize – has now caught on in Australia, New Zealand and parts of the US. In Britain, where pubs are closing at alarming rate, it's often all that's keeping them afloat. And TV quiz shows are enjoyed all over the world, with a new one seemingly appearing each week. The combination of a test of someone's knowledge of trivia with the possibility of winning a life-changing financial reward seems to have a near universal appeal. *Who Wants to be a Millionaire?*, one of the big daddies of the genre, has had versions produced in more than one hundred countries, from Venezuela to the Philippines, India to Australia.

So, we've established that this is a quiz about the world, and that the world, in general, is a great fan of quizzing, but what country or culture was it that gave us the concept of the quiz? Unfortunately, that's not a question we could include in this book, as none of the standard authorities are sure. The Oxford English Dictionary marks the origin of the word as 'unknown', although it does acknowledge the best and most widely known story which is, as is so often the case, the one least likely to be true. It relates that in 1791, a man called Richard Daly, the manager of a Dublin theatre, bet his friends a considerable sum of money that he could, within just 48 hours, get a new, completely made-up word into the vocabulary of the city's inhabitants. To do this, he employed the workers at his theatre to go out into the streets at night, armed with pieces of chalk and write his made-up word, 'QUIZ', onto as many walls, doors, shutters and other visible public surfaces as they could find. When the city awoke, the strange new word became the main topic of conversation, embedding itself in the language and winning Daly his bet. Its mysterious origins gave the word its meaning as people began to describe anything new or unexplained as a 'quiz', from where it took on its modern sense of a set of questions.

It's a good story but almost certainly fabricated. For one thing, it didn't appear in print for the first time until at least 40 years after the event and, perhaps more tellingly, the word quiz already existed in 1791, although it had a rather different meaning to the one it has today. Back then, it was a derogatory term for an overly diligent student, similar to 'swot' or 'nerd'. That the word's meaning evolved from something that mocked study to something that celebrated it isn't too much of a stretch for the imagination, although there's no evidence to show how this might have happened.

Instead, the best guess is the most prosaic one: that it's a simple derivation of 'inquisitive', whose path is much easier to trace – it came into English from the Old French *inquistif*, which was itself derived from the Latin *inquisitivus*. Somewhere along the way, inquisitive also gave rise to a word with much tougher connotations, inquisition, which in the Middle Ages came to mean a trial of one's religious faith that could be the difference between life and death. Sometimes a really testing quiz can feel a bit like that.

Still, if we're not able to define where quizzing came from, we can at least define what it is. It's the joy of recollection and recall, the pleasure of pondering and testing what you know. Sure, there's satisfaction in the immediate answer, the fact brought instantly to mind. But there's perhaps a deeper joy in exploring the forgotten cupboards and dusty cellars of your memory to dig out something you didn't even know you knew. Of course, at times, the cupboard may remain resolutely locked and the answer rooted on the tip of your tongue. It just depends whether the 'right' questions come up.

So, without further delay, let's get quizzing and see if they do. Remember, pub quiz rules apply: no phones, no cheating.

Chapter 1

Day-Tripper
(Easy)

Quiz 1 **Beginning with...**

Let's start off with a few simple questions. To help out,
we've provided the first letter of each answer.

1. What 'L' is the capital and largest city of Peru?

2. Beginning with 'O', what Scandinavian capital city is home to the Munch Museum, the Holmenkollen Ski Museum and the Vigeland Sculpture Park?

3. Which Italian city beginning with 'N' is overlooked by the active volcano, Mt Vesuvius?

4. The Australian marsupials koalas feed almost exclusively on the leaves of which type of tree, beginning with 'E'?

5. What 'L' is a city where the US film industry has been based since the early 20th century?

6. Established in 1872, and straddling the states of Wyoming, Montana and Idaho, what 'Y' was the United States' first national park?

7. What 'P' is an artificial waterway linking the Atlantic and Pacific oceans?

8. The three nations that make up the Low Countries are Belgium, the Netherlands and what other country beginning with 'L'?

9. What 'A' is a European country that has Vienna as its capital?

10. The summit of Mt Everest is on the border of China and which other country beginning with 'N'?

11. What 'E' is an extensive area of tropical wetlands covering the southern tip of the US state of Florida?

12. What 'T', the capital and largest city of its country, is overlooked by Mt Fuji, seen here?

13. Two of Australia's states were named in honour of Queen Victoria. One is Victoria. What is the other? It begins with 'Q'.

14. What 'U' is a taxi-hiring app operating in cities across the world that was founded in 2009?

15. Europe's most sparsely populated country, what 'I' is a volcanic island in the North Atlantic?

16. What 'Z' is the capital and largest city of Croatia?

17. What 'T' is a North African country that lies between Algeria and Libya?

18. What 'I' is the largest city in Turkey?

19. A combination of shellfish and potatoes, what 'M' is considered one of Belgium's national dishes?

20. What country beginning with 'E' is the location of the Great Pyramid of Giza?

© SeanPavonePhoto / Getty Images

Answers on p.42   Score [   ]

Quiz 2 **General Knowledge**

1. The Prado Museum is located in which European city?

2. What is the only continent where you can see meerkats in the wild?

3. The US TV show *Frasier* was set in what US city? And, for a bonus point, where was its forerunner, *Cheers,* set?

4. The Great Red Spot is a giant storm on which planet in our solar system?

5. Which famous Australian bridge is nicknamed the 'Coathanger'?

6. What is the name of the area of geometrically shaped volcanic columns on the north coast of Northern Ireland?
A) The Devil's Causeway
B) The Giant's Causeway
C) The King's Causeway

7. The Smilodon, a prehistoric creature that prowled the Americas from around 2.5 million years ago to 10,000 years ago, had particularly long what?
A) Horns
B) Talons
C) Teeth

8. What is the name of New Zealand's indigenous people?

9. The Giants, the Rangers and the Yankees are sporting teams based in which US city?

10. What is the German word for a motorway or highway?

11. Found in zoos across the world, but only in the wild in China, the panda (or giant panda) is a very fussy eater. What plant makes up over 99% of its diet?

12. The Cape of Good Hope is a rocky headland that lies at the southern tip of which continent?

13. Sunset Boulevard is a major street in which US city?

14. What is the world's second largest hot desert, after the Sahara?
A) The Arabian Desert
B) The Gobi Desert
C) The Great Victoria Desert, Australia

15. Mr Sax's House (La Maison de Monsieur Sax) is a museum dedicated to Adolphe Sax, the inventor of the saxophone. In which European country would you find it?

16. Located in the Indian Ocean, what island nation is the world's lowest-lying country?
A) The Maldives B) Sri Lanka C) Madagascar

17. What is the largest city in South America by population?
A) Buenos Aires, Argentina
B) São Paulo, Brazil
C) Santiago, Chile

18. By what name is Uluru, a large sandstone rock formation in Australia's Northern Territory, also known?

19. In geographical terms, what links these pairs of countries:
· New Zealand and Spain
· Argentina and China
· Fiji and Mali?

20. Can you name the 10 countries that share a border with Brazil? You get a point for each. And, for two bonus points, can you name the only two South American countries that don't share a border with Brazil?

Answers on p.42 Score

Quiz 3 **General Knowledge**

1. How long is the Great Wall of China?
A) 2096 km (1300 miles)
B) 12,096 km (7500 miles)
C) 21,196 km (13,170 miles)

2. What is the nickname of the New Zealand men's rugby union team?

3. And what is the nickname of the New Zealand men's basketball team? (Think about it.)

4. What is the line of latitude 23.5° north of the Equator more commonly known as?
A) Tropic of Cancer B) Tropic of Capricorn

5. What is the name of the mythical 'city of gold' believed by early European explorers to exist somewhere in South America?
A) El Dorado B) Shangri La C) Timbuktu

6. Goulash (or *gulyás*) is the national dish of which European country?

7. In 1927, who became the first person to fly solo non-stop across the Atlantic Ocean?
A) Charles Lindbergh
B) Louis Blériot
C) Richard Branson

8. What is the name of the apple brandy made in northwest France (in a department of the same name)?

9. The primatologist Dian Fossey spent 19 years, from 1966 to 1985, studying the behaviour of which animals in the forests of Rwanda?

10. Dalmatia is a region of which European country?
A) Serbia B) Croatia C) Albania

11. What are the names of the first two humans to walk on the Moon?

12. Kenya's two official languages are English and what else?

13. The TGV is a high-speed intercity rail service in which country? And, for a bonus point, what does TGV stand for?

14. Which US state has the largest population?
A) Alaska B) California C) Florida

15. What city is this?

16. The outbreak of the First World War was precipitated by the assassination of Archduke Franz Ferdinand, the heir to the Austro-Hungarian throne, in which city?

17. Some people believe Mt Ararat in Turkey to be the final resting place of what form of transportation described in the Bible?

18. In what year were the first euro notes and coins introduced?
A) 1961 B) 1996 C) 2001

19. Built during the rule of the Emperor Vespasian in the first century CE, what is the name of the enormous amphitheatre in central Rome, much of which is still standing?

20. Can you name the eight US states that begin with the letter 'M'? You get a point for each.

© Michael Heffernan

Answers on p.42 Score

Quiz 4 **Capital Cities**

See if you can work out the capital cities from the following clues.

1. It hosted the 2008 summer Olympic Games and is home to a palace complex known as the Forbidden City.

2. It's home to the Arc de Triomphe and the Champs-Élyseés.

3. It's situated on the Potomac River and boasts numerous national monuments, including the Lincoln Memorial.

4. It's home to a complex of government buildings called the Kremlin.

5. It lies on the River Plate (*Río de la Plata*) and its name means 'good airs' in English.

6. It was divided by a wall from 1961 to 1989.

7. It's one of the world's most populated cities and provided the setting for the 2003 film *Lost in Translation*.

8. It's on its country's North Island (in the southern hemisphere) and was named after a British 19th-century war hero.

9. It's the birthplace of the playwrights Oscar Wilde, George Bernard Shaw and Samuel Beckett.

10. It's where you can climb the Petronas Towers, the tallest twin towers in the world.

11. It was the site of Plato's Academy, Aristotle's Lyceum and is still overlooked by the Parthenon.

12. It's Europe's lowest capital, at 2 m (6 ft) below sea level.

13. It lies on a Communist-run Caribbean island, just south of the US state of Florida.

14. It's home to a bronze statue of *The Little Mermaid* from the Hans Christian Andersen fairy tale.

15. It was built over the top of the Aztec capital, Tenochtitlán.

16. It's where you can explore Wenceslas Square and the world's largest castle.

17. It's overlooked by Table Mountain.

18. It's on the banks of the River Tagus and boasts districts including Baixa, Belém and the Bairro Alto.

19. It's bordered by Israel and the Palestinian Territories to the east, Sudan to the south and Libya to the east.

20. It's located here:

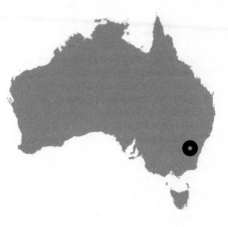

Answers on p.42   Score [ ]

Quiz 5 **General Knowledge**

1. Popular in Central and Eastern European cuisine, sauerkraut is made of fermented what?

2. The 'Socceroos' is the nickname of which country's international football team?

3. Which is the only continent where you can see tigers in the wild?

4. What was the name of the volcano that exploded with deadly force in 1980 in the US state of Washington?

5. What is a gaucho?
A) A cloak worn in North Africa
B) A cold Spanish soup
C) A South American horseman

6. What major waterway and trade route opened on 17 November 1869?

7. Featuring over 53,000 performances of around 3400 shows in 300 venues over the course of 25 days, the world's biggest annual arts festival is held in which British city?

8. Which city has the world's highest number of skyscrapers?
A) Dubai B) New York C) Hong Kong

9. Widely eaten in the southern African countries of Botswana, Namibia, Zimbabwe and South Africa, what is biltong?
A) Dried cured meat B) A spicy soup
C) A bread roll

10. The Earth is one of how many planets in our solar system?
A) Six B) Eight C) Ten

11. Ko Samui, Ko Tao and Phuket are all islands in which Southeast Asian country?
A) Malaysia B) Thailand C) Vietnam

12. What was the surname of the American brothers Dr John Harvey and Will Keith who in 1896 patented a new form of breakfast cereal made of flakes of toasted corn (maize)?

13. There are three copies of Norwegian painter Edvard Munch's best known painting on display in Oslo: two at the Munch Museum and one at the National Gallery of Oslo. What is its name?

14. Name this famous performing arts venue:

15. Usually made of leather or fur, what is the name of the pouch often worn with a kilt as part of traditional Scottish highland dress?

16. What is the currency of Brazil?
A) Deal B) Meal C) Real

17. Found in East Africa, India, Southeast Asia and Australia, what sort of animal is a flying fox?

18. Who is the only US president to have been born outside the US mainland?

19. What was the nickname of Louis XIV, the French monarch behind the enormous Palace of Versailles on the outskirts of Paris?

20. What are the 'Big Five' game animals of Africa – supposedly the five animals that are most difficult to track on foot? You get a point for each.

Answers on p.43   Score

Quiz 6 **General Knowledge**

1. The chemist Cyril Percy Callister invented which spreadable Australian culinary delicacy in 1922?

2. Paris, with a population of roughly 2.2 million people, is France's largest city. But what is its second largest?
A) Toulouse B) Marseille C) Lyon

3. Copacabana is a famous beach and neighbourhood in which South American city?

4. In what country would you find this pyramid?
A) Mexico B) Egypt C) France

5. What is the furthest planet from Earth in our solar system?
A) Uranus B) Neptune C) Pluto

6. If you wanted to take a look at Michelangelo's *The Creation of Adam*, what building should you visit?

7. The city of Fez, after which the famous hat is named, is in which country?
A) Morocco
B) Turkey
C) Egypt

8. Roughly how much of the Earth's surface is covered in water?
A) 51% B) 71% C) 91%

9. The Seychelles are an island nation in which ocean?

10. Who ruled Cuba, first as prime minister then as president, from 1959 until his retirement in 2008?

11. What is the name of the Hindu spring festival, also known as the 'Festival of Colours', in which people cover each other with coloured powders?

12. In Greek mythology, who undertook a quest for the Golden Fleece? And, for a bonus point, what was his boat called?

13. What is the island prison, now a tourist attraction, where the former South African president Nelson Mandela spent 18 of his 27 years in captivity?

14. The Straits of Magellan is a sea passage through which continent?
A) Africa B) Asia C) South America

15. What is the name of the national anthem of Australia?

16. The clarified butter (or butter fat) used widely in Indian cuisine is known as what?

17. Which river flows through the Italian capital of Rome?

18. Weddell, Ross, fur and elephant all are types of what creature found in the waters of Antarctica?

19. In American Football, how many points are awarded for a touchdown?

20. China shares a land border with 14 countries. How many can you name? You get a point for each.

Answers on p.43   Score

Quiz 7 **General Knowledge**

1. What is the world's third largest ocean?

2. What is the capital of South Korea?

3. Where does the world's largest land carnivore live?
A) Africa B) India C) The Arctic Circle

4. The Danish carpenter Ole Kirk Christiansen founded which global toy company?

5. What is the name of the Japanese wine made from fermented rice?

6. In what country did tulips originate?
A) The Netherlands
B) Turkey
C) India

7. What is the tallest mountain in Africa? And, for a bonus point, in what country would you find it?

8. The Philadelphia Eagles play which sport?
A) Baseball
B) American football
C) Basketball

9. What is the longest, and largest, river in South America?

10. The Bass Strait separates mainland Australia from which island, itself a state of Australia?

11. The British Overseas Territory of Gibraltar lies at the southern tip of which European country?

12. The Caribbean island of Puerto Rico belongs to which country?

13. In 1066, the Normans invaded and took over England. From what modern country did the Normans come from?

14. What was the name of Christopher Columbus's flagship on his 1492 journey to the Americas?

15. Now a peaceful square, during the French Revolution the Place de la Concorde was the site of a guillotine where various royals and royalists were executed. In what year did the Revolution begin?
A) 1689
B) 1789
C) 1889

16. Nairobi is the capital and largest city of which African country?
A) Ethiopia
B) Morocco
C) Kenya

17. Name this world-famous landmark?

18. The record label Motown was founded in which US city?
A) New York
B) Detroit
C) Chicago

19. Sumo is a style of wrestling performed in what country?
A) China B) South Korea C) Japan

20. Can you name the four US states that have the word 'New' in their name? You get a point for each.

Answers on p.43   Score

Quiz 8 **Food and Drink**

1. Used widely in Indian cooking, what is a tandoor?
A) A spice
B) An oven
C) A utensil for stirring

2. Produced in the US state of Kentucky, Four Roses, Wild Turkey and Jim Beam are all brands of which distilled spirit?
A) Bourbon
B) Vodka
C) Gin

3. Which two countries claim to have invented the flat white coffee?

4. What mammal, known locally as *cuy* (and pronounced 'kwee'), is a popular dish in the restaurants of Peru?

5. The aniseed-flavoured tipple ouzo is from which country?

6. The Welsh speciality laver bread is made out of oatmeal and which aquatic ingredient?

7. A mixture of meat, vegetables and rice, jambalaya is dish that originated in which US state?

8. Which English county does Wensleydale cheese come from?
A) Yorkshire B) Devon C) Surrey

9. Cinnamon, vanilla and what other spice are often used to flavour eggnog?

10. What is the name of the traditional Greek dish, baked in the oven with aubergines and minced meat?

11. The Indian condiment *raita* consists of vegetables and herbs mixed with what?

12. If someone in Australia offers you a schooner or a pot, what would you expect to receive?
A) A bowl of soup
B) A glass of beer
C) A steak on a plate

13. What is the main ingredient of the Mexican dip guacamole?

14. Leffe is a brand of beer manufactured in which country?
A) Germany B) Belgium C) The Netherlands

15. A type of fish, the sturgeon is the source of which culinary delicacy?

16. What sort of pastry is used to make the honey-drenched and nut-filled dessert baklava, which is eaten across the Balkans, Turkey and the Middle East?

17. The bread known as ciabatta and the sparkling wine prosecco are both from which country?

18. According to the National Turkey Federation, how many turkeys are eaten every year in the US at Thanksgiving?
A) 5 million
B) 25 million
C) 45 million

19. Eaten widely in West Africa, what are the dough balls made of boiled, ground plantain and cassava known as?
A) Bubu
B) Fufu
C) Gugu

20. Hot, spicy Tabasco sauce is produced in which country?
A) Mexico
B) USA
C) Brazil

Answers on p.44 Score

Quiz 9 **General Knowledge**

1. Which US city was once known as New Amsterdam?

2. The Māori name for New Zealand, *Aotearoa*, translates as what?
A) The Land of the Long White Cloud
B) Hobbit Country
C) The Place of Many Islands

3. What city plays host to the world's largest annual carnival?

4. Between 1960 and 1963, prior to their worldwide fame, the Beatles played a series of gigs in the small clubs of which German city?

5. With some examples growing over 115 m (377 ft) high, the coastal redwood is the world's tallest tree. In what country would you find it?

6. What's the name of the style of Chinese food consisting of bite-sized portions served on small plates, or in steamer baskets, and usually with tea?

7. The chihuahua, the smallest breed of dog in the world, originated in which country?

8. What was name of the first artificial satellite, launched by the Soviet Union in 1957?

9. What is the only continent that contains parts of the eastern, western, northern and southern hemispheres?

10. Once the world's tallest free-standing structure, the 553 m-high (1,815 ft) CN Tower is in which Canadian city?

11. What was the name of the defensive fortification begun in 122 CE to mark the northern limit of Roman control in Britain?

12. In what city would you find the world's largest fish market?
A) Sydney, Australia
B) Mexico City, Mexico
C) Tokyo, Japan

13. What is the name of the Paris cemetery, the city centre's largest, where various famous writers, musicians and entertainers, including Oscar Wilde, Jim Morrison and Edith Piaf, are buried?

14. Native to the Americas, what is the third largest of the big cats, after the tiger and lion?

15. In what decade did Hawaii become the 50th US state?
A) 1850s B) 1910s C) 1950s

16. What is the longest river in France?
A) Seine B) Loire C) Thames

17. Having gained independence in 2011, what is the newest country in the world?
A) Eritrea B) Benin C) South Sudan

18. What iconic structure is this?

19. What fictional character lived at 221b Baker Street, London?

20. The Himalayas run through six countries. Can you name them all? You get a point for each.

Answers on p.44   Score

Quiz 10 **General Knowledge**

1. Stromboli and Vesuvius are two of Italy's three active volcanoes. Can you name the third?

2. Andrew Barton 'Banjo' Patterson was the composer of what famous 'bush ballad', sometimes referred to as Australia's unofficial national anthem?

3. The Stanley Cup is an annual championship in which sport, competed for by teams in the USA and Canada?

4. In what continent would you expect to see this road sign?

5. What was the number of the Apollo mission that put the first humans on the Moon?
A) 8 B) 11 C) 17

6. Roughly how much of the world's ice is located in Antarctica?
A) 30% B) 60% C) 90%

7. The Brazilian city of Manaus is surrounded by which natural feature?
A) Cliffs B) Forest C) Desert

8. Having set off from Southampton on England's south coast, to which city was the *Titanic* heading when it sank on its maiden journey?
A) New York B) Miami C) Rio de Janeiro

9. An Italian delicacy, what is mortadella?
A) A cheese B) A sausage C) A wine

10. Which US city's tourist attractions include the Golden Gate Bridge and the former prison of Alcatraz?

11. The flags of Bhutan, Malta and Wales all feature what mythological creature?

12. In what city would you find the Spanish Steps? (Clue: it's not in Spain.)

13. The largest gem-quality rough diamond ever found, the Cullinan diamond, was discovered in which country in 1905?
A) South Africa B) India C) Australia

14. What is the name of the Canadian dish consisting of French fries topped with cheese curds and gravy?

15. What's the capital of Chile?
A) San Jose B) San Juan C) Santiago

16. The Outback is the name of the dry, remote interior of which country?

17. What's the name of the giant limestone statue with the body of a lion and the head of a human that sits on the eastern side of the Pyramid Complex of Giza?

18. Rated by pilots as one of the most dangerous landings in the world, in what country is Tenzing-Hillary Airport?

19. In what country would you find the Mojave Desert?

20. How many of the eight countries to have won the FIFA World Cup can you name? You get a point for each. And can you earn an extra point by naming the only country to have won it five times?

Answers on p.44   Score

Quiz 11 Sports Venues

Take a global sporting tour with this quiz on the
world's greatest stadiums and venues.

1. Wrigley Field is the home of which US
baseball team?
A) New York Yankees
B) Houston Astros
C) Chicago Cubs

2. In what country is Sochi, which was the
venue for the 2014 Winter Olympics?
A) South Korea B) Norway C) Russia

3. The Stade Roland-Garros in Paris hosts
what annual sporting event?
A) The French Open
B) The start of the Tour de France
C) The 24 Hour of Le Mans motor race

4. In what city would you find Hampden Park,
the home of the Scotland football team?
A) Edinburgh
B) Glasgow
C) Perth

5. What major horse race is staged at
Churchill Downs?
A) The Kentucky Derby
B) The Grand National
C) Prix de l'Arc de Triomphe

6. Where does the national football team of
Mexico play its home games?
A) Estadio Mayana
B) Estadio Azteca
C) Estadio Zapoteca

7. What sport is played at Lords in London?
A) Tennis B) Cricket C) Golf

8. Manchester United play their home games
at which stadium?
A) White Hart Lane
B) Anfield
C) Old Trafford

9. The Scotiabank Arena is home to which
Canadian ice hockey team?
A) Toronto Maple Leafs
B) Montreal Canadiens
C) Vancouver Canucks

10. What is the nickname of China's National
Stadium (seen here), which was built for the
2008 Summer Olympics?
A) The Dumpling
B) The Bird's Nest
C) The Big Red

11. In what US city would you find
Dodger Stadium?
A) New York
B) Miami
C) Los Angeles

12. At what venue does the French football
team Paris St-Germain play its home games?
A) Parc des Princes
B) Parc des Reines
C) Parc des Rois

13. The Arthur Ashe Stadium in New York
is the main stadium for what annual
sporting event?
A) The Super Bowl
B) The World Series
C) The US Open

14. The Jawaharlal Nehru Stadium is the national stadium of which country?
A) Russia B) India C) Turkey

15. Where in Scotland would you find the Old Course, considered the world's oldest golf course and the 'home of golf'?
A) Troon
B) Muirfield
C) St Andrews

16. Which US city has staged more world title boxing fights than any other?
A) New York
B) Atlantic City
C) Las Vegas

17. The Gabba is a large cricket ground in which country?
A) Australia
B) New Zealand
C) South Africa

18. In what year did South Africa stage and win the Rugby World Cup, playing the final in front of 60,000 spectators at Johannesburg's Ellis Stadium?
A) 1987
B) 1995
C) 2007

19. Estadio Monumental Antonio Vespucio Liberti is the national football stadium of which South American country?
A) Brazil
B) Chile
C) Argentina

20. The winners of the NBA Championship in 2015, 2017 and 2018, the Golden State Warriors play their home games at the Oracle Arena in which Californian city?
A) Los Angeles
B) Oakland
C) San Francisco

21. In what city is Wembley, the national stadium of England's football team, located?
A) London B) Leeds C) Liverpool

22. The tiny European principality of Monaco stages a major annual event in which sport?
A) Tour de France cycling
B) Formula One motor racing
C) International boules

23. The Camp Nou stadium (seen here) is the home to which of Spain's leading football teams?
A) Barcelona
B) Real Madrid
C) Atlético Madrid

24. Last held in 2018 at the Albatros course at Le Golf National, near Paris, France, the Ryder Cup is a golfing competition staged every two years between which two teams?
A) Europe and Australia
B) USA and UK
C) USA and Europe

25. The New York Knicks play their home games at which famous New York venue?
A) Madison Square Garden
B) Radio City
C) Carnegie Hall

Answers on p.44   Score

Quiz 12 **General Knowledge**

1. The Statue of Liberty was given to the United States by which country?

2. This is the outline of which country?
A) USA B) Russia C) China

3. What is the only large area of land on Earth that is not (officially) owned by any country?

4. What 'lost' city of South America did the American archaeologist Hiram Bingham discover in 1911?

5. Celebrated by Hindus in October or November each year across world, how is the 'Festival of Lights' better known?

6. The Springboks is the nickname of which country's rugby union team?

7. In 1893, what country became the first to give women the vote in parliamentary elections?
A) Canada B) Australia C) New Zealand

8. Which country takes up almost half of South America's land area?

9. What is the capital of Canada?
A) Ottawa B) Montreal C) Toronto

10. The Oktoberfest beer festival is held every year in which German city?

11. Set in the Australian Northern Territory and New York City, what 1980s movie is the highest-grossing Australian film of all time? And, for a bonus point, in what year was it released?

12. How many countries does the US share a land border with, and what are they?

13. In what European country is the Shakespeare play *Hamlet* set?

14. The name of which Central American country translates into English as 'The Saviour'?

15. What colourful sea separates northeast Africa from the Arabian Peninsula?

16. Home to works by Rembrandt, Van Gogh and Vermeer, in which European capital city would you find the Rijksmuseum?

17. Tupelo, Mississippi was the birthplace of which famous 20th-century singer?

18. The 2000 Summer Olympics Games were staged in which southern hemisphere city?
A) Sydney, Australia
B) Johannesburg, South Africa
C) Buenos Aires, Argentina

19. A statue of whom stands on a column at the centre of London's Trafalgar Square?
A) Winston Churchill
B) Lord Horatio Nelson
C) Princess Diana

20. The Chinese Zodiac operates on a 12-year cycle, with a different animal representing each year. How many animals of the Zodiac can you name? You get a point for each – and an extra five points if you list them in the right order.

Answers on p.45   Score

Quiz 13 **General Knowledge**

1. The Lantern Festival marks the final day of which country's New Year celebrations?

2. What is the capital of Mongolia?
A) Mongolia City
B) Beijing
C) Ulaanbaatar (or Ulan Bator)

3. What is New Zealand's national bird?

4. What is the name of the area near the ancient Egyptian city of Thebes where over 60 pharaohs were buried in tombs carved out of the rock?

5. What is the largest country in the world by area?
A) China
B) Australia
C) Russia

6. What gin-based cocktail was invented at the Raffles Hotel, Singapore, in the early 20th century?

7. Count Dracula was from Transylvania, a historic region in which modern country?

8. A cross between a grizzly bear and a polar bear is called a pizzly bear; true or false?

9. Old Faithful is the name of a what in the USA's Yellowstone Park?

10. What European country is nicknamed the 'boot' owing to its distinctive shape?

11. Originating in West Africa, what is a *djembe*?
A) A vegetable stew
B) A dance
C) A type of drum

12. What's the official language of Brazil?

13. Founded in 1718, which US city is nicknamed the 'Big Easy'?

14. What is the only continent where the spectacled bear can be seen in the wild?

15. The Virgin Islands in the Caribbean are divided between which two countries?
A) The Netherlands and France
B) France and USA
C) USA and UK

16. Can you put these three cities in size order by population?
A) Paris B) Rome C) Berlin

17. The MCG, the southern hemisphere's largest sports venue, is in which city?

18. In what European country is there no legally enforced speed limit on many of the highways?

19. What New York location (below) has been given the nicknames the 'Crossroads of the World', the 'Centre of the Universe' and 'The Heart of the Great White Way'?

20. Can you name the top 10 most spoken languages in the world (in terms of the number of native speakers), according to the figures published by the language research organisation, Ethnologue? You get a point for each.

© Marco Rubino / Shutterstock

Answers on p.45   Score

Quiz 14 **General Knowledge**

1. What is the most visited museum in the world?
A) Louvre, Paris, France
B) National Museum of Natural History, Washington DC, USA
C) National Museum of China, Beijing, China

2. Area 51, the highly restricted US Air Force facility (and supposed repository of captured alien technology), is in which US state?

3. If you were in South America and were invited to have a *mate* ('mah-tay'), what would you be being asked to do?

4. Whose portrait adorns the currencies of both Australia and New Zealand?

5. Originating in Andalusia, what is the name of the Spanish soup made of blended vegetables and served cold?

6. 'The Windy City' is the nickname of which US city?

7. The world's largest species of lizard can be found on – and is named after – which Indonesian island?

8. Boca Juniors soccer team play in which South American city?
A) Caracas
B) São Paulo
C) Buenos Aires

9. What four countries make up the United Kingdom? You get a point for each.

10. By what nickname are the Royal Canadian Mounted Police often known?

11. St Mark's Square (Piazza San Marco) is the main public square, and one of the major tourist draws, in which Italian city?

12. On what date do Australians celebrate Australia Day?

13. In what US state would you find the theme parks Disney World and Universal Orlando?

14. What is a yurt?
A) A circular tent used by nomadic peoples of Central Asia
B) A Pakistani unit of currency
C) A Chinese cheese made from panda milk

15. What is Africa's largest lake, covering an area of around 969,215 sq km (26,724 miles)?

16. The national flag of which country is made up of a yellow cross on a blue background?
A) Norway B) Sweden C) Greece

17. What is the large thorny Southeast Asian fruit that has such a strong odour it is banned in Singapore's hotels and on its public transportation system?

18. According to tradition, Betsy Ross of Philadelphia, Pennsylvania, came up with what in 1776?
A) The American anthem, 'The Star Spangled Banner'
B) The first American flag, the Stars and Stripes
C) The official recipe for America's favourite dessert, apple pie

19. Developed in Cuba in the early 20th century, what are the two main ingredients of a Cuba Libre cocktail?

20. Can you name the world's 10 most traded currencies (according to research by the Bank of International Settlements)? You get a point for each.

Answers on p.45   Score

Quiz 15 **Guess the City**

See if you can work out the city from these clues.

1. Out in the middle of a desert, this city is a popular place to get married, to watch a show, to win (or lose) a fortune and to stay in some of the biggest hotels in the world which line its glitzy neon-lit main street.

2. The coastal *Cidade Maravilhosa* ('Marvellous City') is overlooked by Sugarloaf Mountain and is its country's second largest city. Every year it stages a major samba-themed celebration at the start of Lent.

3. This European capital is super bike-friendly with over half of the population cycling to work. It's home to the amusement park Tivoli Gardens, as well as a flagship store of one of the country's most famous companies, Lego.

4. Founded next to one of the world's great rivers, and one of the Seven Wonders of the Ancient World, this city's main museum contains treasures from the ancient civilisation that thrived here thousands of years ago, including gold death masks and enormous sarcophagi.

5. Straddling two continents, either side of a narrow stretch of water, this was once the capital of a mighty empire that stretched across the Middle East, North Africa and Eastern Europe. Today, it's home to over 3000 mosques, five major soccer teams and an enormous Grand Bazaar.

6. The most highly populated city in Oceania with over five million inhabitants, this area has been inhabited for over 30,000 years. The first European settlers arrived in the 1770s to found a penal colony from which the city grew. It's famed for its opera house, sporting venues and has hosted the Summer Olympics.

7. Founded in 1642, this mostly French-speaking city has a name that means 'royal mountain' and was once a major centre for fur trading. Today it boasts one of the world's biggest bug zoos, the Insectarium, and its basilica holds North America's largest bell.

8. Home of the intense dance known as the tango, this city has more bookshops per person than any other. Its famous sights include a large above-ground cemetery, La Recoleta, where various notable figures, including former first lady Eva Maria Duarte de Perón (better known as Evita), are buried.

9. Sat beneath an extinct volcano called Arthur's Seat, this city also boasts a castle and a palace. Its main roads are the Royal Mile and Princes Street where the locals gather on New Year's Eve to celebrate with a raucous party known as Hogmanay.

10. Overlooked by a snow-capped mountain, this capital of an island nation forms part of the world's most populous metropolitan area, home to more than 30 million people. Its major industries include electronics, publishing and broadcasting.

11. The world's longest train service starts from here, not far from the city's central Red Square. The former headquarters of a powerful communist empire, it's famed for its beautiful metro stations and renowned ballet company, based at the Bolshoi Theatre.

12. Built beside one of world's largest natural harbours, next to the Blue Mountains, this is the largest (mainly) English-speaking city south of the USA. One of its most famous neighbourhoods is Trenchtown, as sung about by the reggae musician, Bob Marley.

Answers on p.46   Score

Quiz 16 **General Knowledge**

1. What are the Nazca Lines?
A) A racing circuit in Indiana, USA
B) A series of giant pictures etched in the desert of southern Peru
C) A mountain range that runs across central Mexico

2. Dingoes are a type of dog native to which country?

3. In the original 1933 film, what New York building did King Kong climb?

4. Which popular drink's name comes from the German word for 'warehouse'?
A) Fanta B) Lager C) Pepsi

5. The Swiss electrical engineer George de Mestral is best known for inventing what type of fastening in the 1950s, which has been a boon to outdoor sports enthusiasts ever since?

6. The State Hermitage Museum is located in which city?

7. Native to Africa, what is the world's largest bird?

8. In 1871, a devastating fire in which US city was supposedly caused by a cow kicking over a lantern?

9. In 1805, the Irish scientist Francis Beaufort devised a 13-point scale (0 to 12) for measuring what natural phenomenon?

10. What was the name of the luxury train service that ceased operating in 2009, but which, at its peak, ran regular timetabled trains between Paris and Constantinople?

11. Fado is a traditional, mournful music from which country?

12. In what country was silk invented?

13. The Abominable Snowman, or yeti, is supposedly a native of which mountain range?

14. In what state is the southernmost point of the continental United States?
A) California
B) Texas
C) Florida

15. What sort of animal was the first living creature to orbit the Earth? And, for a bonus point, what was its name?

16. What is by far the biggest city in Africa with an estimated population of over 17 million people?

17. Coloured red, white and blue, this is the flag of which country?

18. Famed for their ability to 'play dead' when threatened, what is the only type of marsupial found in the Americas?

19. What French city plays host to a major international film festival each year?

20. How many of the seven South American countries that contain parts of the Andes can you name? You get a point for each.

Answers on p.46   Score

Quiz 17 **General Knowledge**

1. What is the capital of the Philippines?
A) Hanoi
B) Manila
C) Bangkok

2. What is the name of the Mexican festival that takes place from 31 October to 2 November, when people get together to remember friends and family members who have passed away?

3. Now a permanently moored tourist attraction in Leith, Edinburgh, what is the name of the former royal yacht of Queen Elizabeth II, which operated from 1954 to 1997?

4. In Australia, what is a Lamington?
A) A large wide-brimmed hat
B) A make of four-wheel drive car
C) A type of sponge cake

5. The Amazon River flows into what ocean?

6. From 1936 to 1941, Ethiopia was occupied by which European country?
A) France
B) Germany
C) Italy

7. The Space Needle and the Museum of Pop Culture are among the tourist attractions of which US city?

8. Leatherback, green, loggerhead and hawksbill are all species of what sort of ocean-going creature?

9. Mambo and cha-cha-cha are dance styles that originated in what Caribbean country?
A) Cuba
B) Dominican Republic
C) Trinidad and Tobago

10. What is the smallest US state?

11. What is the name of the island nation off the southeast coast of India?

12. The Brazilian footballer Edson Arantes do Nascimento is better known by what much shorter name?

13. The Rialto is a bridge in which Italian city?
A) Florence
B) Venice
C) Rome

14. Which famous mountaineer was born in the New Zealand city of Auckland in 1908?

15. Dedicated to the Hindu god Ganesha, the Shree Siddhivinayak Ganapati Mandir is a temple in Mumbai, India. Ganesha has the head of which animal?

16. Who was the first person to travel into space in 1961?

17. What natural wonder are these people gazing out over?

18. The French capital, Paris, is situated on which river?
A) Rhine B) Tiber C) Seine

19. Żubrówka or 'Bison Grass Vodka' is produced in which country?
A) Poland B) Russia C) Sweden

20. New York's Metropolitan Museum is often known by what shorter name?

Answers on p.46   Score

Quiz 18 General Knowledge

1. The three waterfalls, Horseshoe Falls, American Falls and Bridal Falls, are more commonly known by what collective name?

2. What two colours are used on the flag of China?

3. Acapulco is a coastal resort city in which country?

4. The name 'America' is derived from which Italian explorer?

5. What North African stew is named after the earthenware pot in which it is cooked?

6. What is the only great ape that doesn't live in Africa? And in what two countries does it live (a point for each)?

7. What is the world's longest river?
A) Nile B) Yangtze C) Mississippi

8. In which country was *The Lord of the Rings* trilogy filmed?

9. Which US city has sports teams called the Chargers, the Lakers and the Galaxy?

10. Which of these animals is found only in Africa?
A) Leopard B) Elephant C) Zebra
D) Rhinoceros E) Buffalo

11. The French liqueur Cointreau is flavoured with what fruit?

12. In what fictional town in the US state of Kansas did Superman grow up?

13. What is India's currency?

14. The city of London, England, lies on which river?

15. In Australia, someone from Sydney is known as a what?
A) A Sydinkum
B) A Sydnoser
C) A Sydneysider

16. What name is given to the devastating plague that wiped out over a third of Europe's population between 1347 and 1351?

17. What city is this?
A) Seville B) Athens C) Venice

18. The International Date Line passes through the middle of which ocean?

19. If you were looking at the *Mona Lisa* by Leonardo da Vinci, in what museum would you be standing?

20. From what country do the following pop artists come from? You get a point for each.
A) Abba
B) Bjork
C) Bob Marley
D) Daft Punk
E) Dana International
F) Drake
G) Lorde
H) Psy
I) Rihanna
J) Shakira
K) Sia
L) U2

Quiz 19 **Wildlife Around the World**

1. Found on the savannahs of southern Africa, what is the fastest land animal on Earth?

2. What is the largest species of penguin?
A) Adelie B) Humboldt C) Emperor

3. Found on every continent except Antarctica, what is the world's fastest bird?
A) Spine-tailed swift B) Ostrich
C) Peregrine falcon

4. The largest eyes in the animal kingdom belong to what?
A) Blue whale B) Giant squid
C) African elephant

5. What distinguishes monotremes, such as the platypus and echidna of Australia, from all other types of mammal?
A) They lay eggs B) They don't have any hair
C) They only have one eye

6. What type of animal is a boomslang?
A) Fish B) Bird C) Snake

7. Found in northern latitudes across the world, caribou are commonly known by what other name?

8. *Dà xióng māo*, meaning 'big bear cat', is the Chinese name for which animal?

9. What is the name of the sharp-toothed fish that live in schools in the rivers of South America and are famed for their aggressive predatory behaviour?

10. The only lizard that forages for vegetation on the sea floor, marine iguanas are found on what tropical island group?

11. Which is the only one of these animals that isn't a marsupial?
A) Tasmanian devil B) Wombat C) Dingo

12. Krill are one of the most abundant creatures on earth, fed on by a great many different species, from fish to whales. What sort of animals are krill?
A) Crustaceans B) Sponges C) Fish

13. What is the name of the order of lizards, found throughout Africa, that are famed for their long tongues, eyes that can move independently of each other and (in some species) the ability to change colour?

14. A (considerably) larger relative of the domestic cat, the puma or mountain lion inhabits much of the Americas. By what other common name does it go by?

15. Found in southern Africa, southern weaver birds are famed for what?
A) Building the largest nests of any birds
B) Forming the largest flocks of any bird
C) Having the loudest cry of any bird

16. The only wild monkeys in Europe live on what small piece of territory?
A) Gibraltar B) Malta C) The Vatican

17. Once known only from fossils and believed to have gone extinct with the dinosaurs 65 million years ago, coelacanths were discovered alive and well in 1939. What sort of animal is a coelocanth?

18. How many vertebrae are there in a giraffe's neck?
A) More than a human
B) Less than a human
C) The same as a human

19. The large marine mammals, manatees, are sometimes known by what name, a reference to their slow, plant-eating lifestyle?

20. What colour is octopus blood?
A) Blue B) Red C) Yellow

Answers on p.47   Score

Quiz 20 **General Knowledge**

1. Striped, brown and spotted (also known as 'laughing') are all species of what African mammal?

2. In what mountain range would you find Mont Blanc? And, for two bonus points, can you name the two countries on whose border it sits?

3. In what city can you visit Paisley Park, the former home and recording studio of the late US musician, Prince?
A) New York B) Los Angeles C) Minneapolis

4. Released in 1934, the 'Surgeon's Photograph' was supposedly an image of which famous Scottish tourist attraction?

5. The Nullarbor Plain is an extremely arid coastal region in which country?

6. What draws tourists to the pavement outside the TLC Chinese Theatre (also known as Grauman's Chinese Theatre) in Los Angeles?

7. K-Pop is a form of pop music from which country?

8. The unfinished cathedral La Sagrada Família is in which European city? And, for a bonus point, who designed it?

9. What sturdy, hard-wearing type of cloth is named after the French town of Nîmes?

10. In what city would you find a huge exhibition space known as the Sambadrome?

11. The Whispering Gallery is a feature of which major London landmark, which was rebuilt by Sir Christopher Wren in the late 17th century after the Great Fire of London?

12. The ecosystem known as savannah, which covers much of sub-Saharan Africa, is made up mainly of what types of plant?

13. Caledonia was the Roman name for which country of the United Kingdom?

14. What is the name of the Mexican dish consisting of minced spiced meat in cornmeal dough cooked in a maize husk?

15. The extinct human species Neanderthals were named after the Neander Valley where the first fossils were found. In what country is the Neander Valley?

16. Tierra del Fuego, the 'Land of Fire', is a province in which South American country?

17. The Gobi Desert stretches across northern China and what other Asian country?

18. The 8 km (5 mile) Øresund Bridge (below) connects which two Scandinavian cities (and countries)?

19. What is the name of the fault (a boundary between two tectonic plates) that runs for around 1200 km (750 miles) through the US state of California?

20. Can you name the six states of Australia (a point for each)?

© Aeronautics / Shutterstock

Answers on p.47   Score

Quiz 21 **General Knowledge**

1. Pyongyang is the capital and largest city of which communist-run Asian country?

2. Found mainly in the Arctic Ocean, what colour are beluga whales?
A) Grey B) Pink C) White

3. New York City's theatre district is centred on which wide street?

4. Meanwhile, across the Atlantic, the West End is a nickname for the theatre district of which European city?

5. In what country was the 2010 FIFA World Cup held, the first time the tournament had been staged on that continent?

6. What's the most northerly country where you can see tigers in the wild?
A) Japan B) Russia C) India

7. Shylock is a character that features in a Shakespeare play set in which European city?

8. In the early 20th century, over 3250 km (2000 miles) of fences were built in Western Australia to stop the spread of which animal?
A) Platypuses
B) Wallabies
C) Rabbits

9. Ketch, cutter, sloop and junk are all types of what form of transport?

10. Which US city dyes its river green every year as part of its St Patrick's Day celebrations on 17 March?

11. Algiers is the capital of which North African country?

12. In what European capital city could you visit the Van Gogh Museum?

13. The festival of Cinco de Mayo celebrates the culture of which country?

14. Put these three cities in size order according to their population, largest first:
A) Tokyo
B) Mexico City
C) New York

15. Easter Island is a territory of which country?
A) Australia
B) USA
C) Chile

16. The Chinese city of Canton is now more commonly known as what?
A) Beijing
B) Guangzhou
C) Shanghai

17. What is the name of the black panther in Rudyard Kipling's *The Jungle Book*?

18. Found lurking in the Amazon jungle, what is the largest spider in the world?
A) The red-kneed tarantula
B) The goliath birdeater
C) The black widow

19. What is this world-famous monument?

20. In what country was Milka chocolate originally made?
A) Switzerland B) Germany C) Ireland

Answers on p.47   Score

Quiz 22 **Country Club**

Can you name each of the 20 countries that have been highlighted on this map of the world from the three options given?

1. A) Canada B) Greenland C) USA
2. A) Jamaica B) Cuba C) Mexico
3. A) Panama B) Venezuela C) Colombia
4. A) Argentina B) Brazil C) Canada
5. A) Norway B) Iceland C) Greenland

6. A) England B) Ireland C) France
7. A) The Netherlands B) Sweden C) Finland
8. A) Scotland B) Poland C) Germany
9. A) Portugal B) Spain C) Greece
10. A) Italy B) Morocco C) Algeria

11. A) Saudi Arabia **B)** Turkey **C)** Egypt
12. A) Ukraine **B)** Nigeria **C)** Kenya
13. A) South Africa **B)** Angola **C)** Sri Lanka
14. A) Zambia **B)** Madagascar **C)** Maldives
15. A) Vietnam **B)** Pakistan **C)** India

16. A) Mongolia **B)** Russia **C)** China
17. A) South Korea **B)** Thailand **C)** Cambodia
18. A) Philippines **B)** Bhutan **C)** Japan
19. A) Papua New Guinea **B)** Nepal **C)** Laos
20. A) Australia **B)** New Zealand **C)** Vanuatu

Answers on p.48   Score

Quiz 23 General Knowledge

1. This is the flag of which country?

2. Roe, red, fallow, sika and sambar are all species of what sort of animal, found throughout the Americas and Eurasia?

3. The leader of the Tour de France wears what colour jersey?
A) Green B) Yellow C) Black

4. If you were attending a concert at Carnegie Hall, in what city would you be in?

5. The Great Barrier Reef, the world's largest coral reef system, lies off the coast of which country?

6. The Chinese-American architect I.M. Pei designed a glass pyramid in 1989 for the courtyard of which famous museum?
A) British Museum, London
B) National Museum of China, Beijing
C) Louvre, Paris

7. What is the national animal of India?
A) Peacock B) Lion C) Tiger

8. Which country lost the FIFA World Cup Final in both 1974 and 1978?

9. Can you name the 14th-century bridge that crosses the Vltava River in Prague and is one of the city's top tourist attractions?
A) Henry Bridge B) George Bridge
C) Charles Bridge

10. Coffee is believed to have originated in which country?
A) Brazil B) Ethiopia C) Italy

11. What was the name of the ship on which a famous mutiny took place near Tahiti in 1787?

12. In 1610, what Italian astronomer and scientist became the first person to observe Jupiter through a telescope, discovering the planet's four largest moons in the process?

13. Followers of the Islamic Mevlevi Order in Konya, Turkey, are more commonly known by what name, a reference to how they spin around while performing their ceremonies?

14. If you were flying from the USA to Italy, using airports with the codes BOS and FLR, which two cities would you be flying between?

15. Found in warm seas across the world, what is the world's largest fish?

16. The constellation Crux is more commonly known by what two-word name?
A) Pole Star B) Southern Cross
C) Asteroid Belt

17. In his thirties, the future leader of a major world power, Iosif Vissarionovich Dzhugashvili from Georgia, adopted what new, metallic-tinged name?

18. In what Italian city would you find the Uffizi Gallery?

19. What is the largest country, by population, that drives on the left?

20. Can you name all nine countries that contain parts of the Amazon rainforest? You get a point for each.

Answers on p.48   Score

Quiz 24 General Knowledge

1. Which is further north, Rome or New York?

2. What is the largest island in Africa?

3. As specified in the Book of Genesis, what mode of transport was 300 cubits long, 50 cubits wide and 30 cubits high?

4. What is the largest river in the world in terms of the volume of water that it carries?
A) Nile B) Amazon C) Mississippi

5. What is gumbo and in what US state did it originate?

6. What is Africa's most dangerous animal?

7. What is Africa's most dangerous large animal?

8. The historic water pageant known as the *Regata Storica* takes place on the Grand Canal of which European city?

9. A major New York tourist attraction, what does MOMA stand for?

10. Which of these cities has the largest population?
A) Sydney, Australia
B) Singapore
C) Kuala Lumpur, Malaysia

11. What is the world's largest species of marsupial?
A) The grey kangaroo
B) The red kangaroo
C) The hairy-nosed wombat

12. The 'crookedest street in the world', which includes a steep section boasting eight hairpin turns on one block, Lombard Street is a tourist attraction in which US city?

13. Indira Gandhi (1917–84) was the first (and so far only female) prime minister of which country?
A) India
B) Australia
C) UK

14. What is the name of the mountain range beginning with 'A' that stretches across much of North Africa?

15. What ancient wonder is this?

16. El Clásico is a football match between which two teams?

17. Valletta is the capital of which European island nation?

18. Africa takes up roughly how much of the world's total land area?
A) 10% B) 20% C) 30%

19. Particularly associated with the Lake District of northwest England where she spent much of her life, what was the name of the author behind such books as *The Tale of Peter Rabbit* and *The Tale of Squirrel Nutkin*?

20. Can you name the only two countries that have hosted the men's World Cups for football, cricket and rugby union?

Quiz 25 **General Knowledge**

1. What (nearly) annual five-day music festival takes place near Pilton in Somerset, England?

2. The silver fern motif is associated with which country, featuring on its coat of arms as well as on the uniforms of many of its sports teams?

3. Bengal, Siberian and Malayan are subspecies of which large Asian animal?

4. Catherine the Great was the ruler of which country in the 18th century?

5. On what continent would you find the Zambezi river?
A) South America B) Africa C) Asia

6. Fondue is a national dish of which European country?

7. What is the capital of Cuba?

8. What's the name of the people indigenous to northern Sweden, Norway and Finland, many of whom are nomadic reindeer herders?

9. What is the most widely spoken language in Argentina?

10. Native to Indonesia, cinnamon is a spice obtained from what part of the *Cinnamomum* tree?
A) Leaves B) Bark C) Seeds

11. Famed for its amusement parks, Coney Island is a beach neighbourhood of which US city?
A) Miami B) Los Angeles C) New York

12. In what country would you find the ruins of the ancient Karnak temple complex?
A) Egypt B) Russia C) China

13. The Thai island of Khao Phing Kan, shown here, is commonly known by what name after its appearance in a 1970s film?
A) Jaws Island B) James Bond Island
C) Rocky Island

14. According to the proverb, 'all roads lead to' what city?

15. The flags of the US, UK, France and Australia are all combinations of what three colours?

16. What is the currency of Canada?
A) Canadian pound
B) Canadian franc
C) Canadian dollar

17. What is the only major city in Australia not located on the coast?
A) Sydney B) Perth C) Canberra

18. What body of water separates Britain from Ireland?
A) The English Channel
B) The Irish Sea
C) The Black Sea

19. The cities of Seville, Granada, Córdoba and Cádiz can all be found in which southern region of Spain?

20. Which of these countries celebrates New Year first?
A) Japan B) New Zealand C) Australia

© Dan Rata / Shutterstock

Answers on p.49   Score

Quiz 26 **General Knowledge**

1. Which of these continents has the smallest number of active volcanoes?
A) North America B) Africa C) Australia

2. In what city would you find the headquarters of the United Nations?
A) Geneva, Switzerland
B) New York, USA
C) Brussels, Belgium

3. Served as snack in Italy, what are arancini?
A) Oranges B) Pizza slices C) Rice balls

4. The Galápagos Islands belong to which country?
A) Chile B) Ecuador C) USA

5. What is the holiest city in Islam?
A) Mecca B) Medina C) Jerusalem

6. What is the largest land animal on Earth?
A) Indian elephant
B) African elephant
C) White rhinoceros

7. Which river forms part of the boundary between the USA and Canada?
A) Mississippi
B) Colorado
C) St Lawrence

8. The Torres del Paine is one of the most visited national parks in which mountainous South American country?

9. What number is considered unlucky in China and several other Asian countries?
A) 1 B) 4 C) 13

10. What is the name of the day of remembrance held on 25 April to honour members of the Australian and New Zealand armed forces who have died in military campaigns?

11. What is the capital of Ukraine?

12. Which European country is the largest, by area?
A) France B) Spain C) Germany

13. Who is the planet Venus named after?
A) The Roman goddess of love
B) The Greek god of the sea
C) The Hindu god of the sky

14. Which of these African countries doesn't have a coastline?
A) South Africa B) Egypt C) Ethiopia

15. The people who live in this country call it *Nippon*. What do we call it?

16. Which of these nations does not have an official national day?
A) USA B) UK C) France

17. In 2011, a devastating earthquake hit which New Zealand city?

18. What is the main religion of Sri Lanka?
A) Hinduism
B) Buddhism
C) Islam

19. In what sea is this person floating?

20. These day, most authorities define Scandinavia as being made up of which five countries? You get a point for each.

Quiz 27 **Silhouette Cities**

This round is simple – just identify which city these silhouette
compilations of major landmarks represent from the three available options.

1.

A) London B) Singapore C) Sydney

4

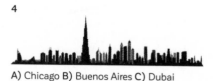

A) Chicago B) Buenos Aires C) Dubai

2.

A) Madrid B) Toronto C) Kuala Lumpur

5.

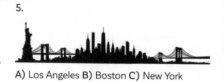

A) Los Angeles B) Boston C) New York

3.

A) Auckland B) Sydney C) Beijing

6.

A) Amsterdam B) Paris C) Prague

7.

A) Kuala Lumpur B) Shanghai C) Delhi

10

A) Cairo B) Marrakesh C) Athens

8.

A) Nairobi B) Naples C) Tokyo

11.

A) Mexico City B) Rio de Janeiro C) Caracas

9.

A) Stockholm B) Moscow C) Helsinki

12.

A) Lisbon B) Rome C) Barcelona

© Shutterstock

Answers on p.49   Score

Quiz 28 **General Knowledge**

1. What tyre company produces an internationally renowned series of restaurant guides, in which outstanding establishments are awarded up to three stars?
A) Pirelli B) Michelin C) Dunlop

2. What is the name of the pilgrimage to Mecca that all Muslims are supposed to undertake once in their lifetime (if they are physically and financially able to do so)?

3. Botany Bay is an area of which Australian city?

4. The Japanese dish of small balls or rolls of vinegar-flavoured cold rice is known as what?

5. La Scala is an opera house situated in which Italian city?

6. One of the largest insects in the world, the goliath beetle is native to which continent?

7. The Major League Baseball season culminates each autumn in a series of games known as what?

8. The skyscraper that stands at 30 St Mary Axe in the City of London is better known by what nickname, also the name of a pickled vegetable?

9. What is the currency of Turkey?
A) The shekel
B) The drachma
C) The lira

10. What major sea separates Europe from Africa?

11. Possibly invented in China, Turkey or Spain (nobody is completely sure), marzipan is a sweet confection made of sugar (or honey) and what other nutty ingredient?

12. Which of these South American countries is largest, by area?
A) Chile B) Peru C) Argentina

13. What is the region of southeastern France famed for its lavender and sunflower fields?

14. What is the biblical-sounding name of the collection of limestone stacks off the coast of Port Campbell National Park in Victoria, Australia?

15. In what sea does the island of Jamaica lie?
A) Dead Sea B) Caribbean Sea C) Baltic Sea

16. Cartagena is a major port in which country?
A) Mexico B) Colombia C) Russia

17. What is the official language of the Canadian province of Québec?
A) English B) French C) Spanish

18. Odessa is a Ukrainian port on which body of water?
A) Black Sea B) Sargasso Sea C) Yellow River

19. What is this ancient monument found on Salisbury Plain in southwest England?

20. What was the largest empire in history?
A) British Empire
B) Spanish Empire
C) Mongol Empire

© William Toti / 500px

Quiz 29 **General Knowledge**

1. Owing to the large number of computer and tech companies located there, including Apple, Intel and Hewlett Packard, by what name is the Santa Clara Valley in the San Francisco Bay Area more usually known?

2. A refuge for lions, elephants, hippos, cheetahs and many other animals, Kruger National Park is in which country?
A) Kenya B) South Africa C) India

3. Eaten throughout the Indian subcontinent, what sort of foodstuff is a roti?
A) A vegetable dumpling
B) A round flatbread C) A lentil curry

4. Stretching for over 5600 km (3400 miles) and designed to protect sheep from attacks by wild dogs, the longest fence in the world was built in the 1880s across which country?
A) South Africa B) USA C) Australia

5. What is the name of the sea that separates Egypt from Saudi Arabia?
A) Blue Sea B) Red Sea C) Green Sea

6. If your plane ticket has you down as travelling from SEA to SYD, between which two cities are you flying?

7. The *Mauer* is the German word for which iconic structure?

8. In the traditional Japanese dance drama, kabuki, all the parts are played by who?
A) Men B) Women C) Puppets

9. Which planet is closest in size to the Earth?
A) Venus B) Mars C) Jupiter

10. In what country would you find Pamukkale ('cotton castle' in the local language), known for its rolling white terraces of calcium carbonate, formed by mineral-rich springs?
A) UK B) France C) Turkey

11. Now an entertainment and concert venue, what was the original name of the giant dome-shaped marquee built for the year 2000 celebrations in North Greenwich, London?

12. Juan Domingo Perón was elected president of which South American country three times?

13. In what country would you find the Franz Josef Glacier and the Fox Glacier?
A) Canada B) India C) New Zealand

14. Which of these rivers empties into the Gulf of Mexico?
A) Mississippi B) Amazon C) Colorado

15. Site of the pyramids of the Sun and Moon, in what country would you find the ancient city of Teotihuacán?
A) Australia B) Mexico C) Egypt

16. Which of Europe's capital cities was largely destroyed by an earthquake in 1755?
A) Lisbon B) Rome C) London

17. What is the name of the river that flows through India and Bangladesh, discharging into the Bay of Bengal, and is considered holy by Hindus?

18. Consisting of wheat noodles in broth, ramen is a dish from which country?
A) Italy B) Japan C) South Africa

19. What is the only country that occupies an entire continent?

20. What birds are traditionally associated with the Tower of London? According to legend, if they ever leave the tower, the country will fall.
A) Ravens B) Owls C) Pigeons

Answers on p.50   Score

Quiz 30 **General Knowledge**

1. Where would you find the seas of Tranquillity and Nectar?

2. The Meeting of the Waters (*Encontro das Águas* in the local language) is the confluence of the dark waters of the Rio Negro with the white waters of what famous river?
A) Thames, England B) Mississippi, USA
C) Amazon, Brazil

3. The Chicxulub crater, believed to have been made by the impact of the asteroid that wiped out the dinosaurs 65 million years ago, is on the coast of which country?
A) Germany B) Mexico C) India

4. What globally famous beverage was invented in 1896 as a tonic wine, or patent medicine, by Confederate Colonel John Pemberton in Columbus, Georgia?
A) Coca-cola B) Pepsi C) Dr Pepper

5. A popular food in Italy, what is a calzone?
A) A stuffed mushroom
B) A prosciutto sandwich C) A folded pizza

6. What country has the greatest surface area of water?
A) Canada B) Brazil C) Saudi Arabia

7. The Spanish Riding School where Lipizzan horses are trained in dressage is in which European capital city? (Clue: it's not in Spain.)

8. By population, what is the largest city, Cairo or Johannesburg?

9. What country's name is derived from the Latin for 'south'?
A) Australia B) Argentina C) Namibia

10. If you're attending an *asado* in Argentina, what sort of food would you be served?
A) Grilled meats B) Cheese sandwiches
C) A light salad

11. Situated next to London Bridge station, the UK's tallest building goes by what sharp-sounding name?

12. Until he was overthrown in 2011, Colonel Gaddafi was the dictator of which country?

13. Which of these countries is not in South America?
A) Chile B) Suriname C) Honduras

14. The Russian port of Vladivostok lies next to which ocean?

15. What is the largest country in the Middle East, by area?
A) Saudi Arabia B) Iran C) Egypt

16. And what is the largest country in the Middle East, by population?
A) Saudi Arabia B) Iran C) Egypt

17. Heathrow Airport serves which major European city?

18. In what Australian state would you find Cradle Mountain, one of the country's top tourist sites?

19. Which famous writer is associated with this building?

© Ron Ellis / Shutterstock

20. What colours are the five rings of the Olympic flag? You get an extra five points if you can identify the order of the colours as they appear from left to right.

Chapter 1

Answers

Answers

Quiz 1
Beginning With...
1. Lima
2. Oslo
3. Naples
4. Eucalyptus
5. Los Angeles
6. Yellowstone
7. Panama Canal
8. Luxembourg
9. Austria
10. Nepal
11. Everglades
12. Tokyo
13. Queensland
14. Uber
15. Iceland
16. Zagreb
17. Tunisia
18. Istanbul
19. *Moules-frites* (mussels and fries)
20. Egypt

Quiz 2
1. Madrid, Spain
2. Africa. They're found in the Kalahari and Namib deserts of southern Africa.
3. *Frasier* was set in Seattle. *Cheers* was set in Boston.
4. Jupiter. The storm has a diameter bigger than the Earth and has been raging for at least 200 years.
5. Sydney Harbour Bridge
6. B) The Giant's Causeway, which, according to legend, was built by the giant Fionn mac Cumhaill.
7. C) Teeth, specifically its canine teeth, which could grow up to 28 cm (11 in), giving rise to the animal's more common name: the sabre-toothed tiger.

8. Māori
9. New York, representing the city in American football, ice hockey and baseball, respectively.
10. Autobahn
11. Bamboo
12. Africa
13. Los Angeles
14. A) The Arabian Desert
15. Belgium, in the city of Dinant.
16. A) The Maldives. No point on any of the 1200 islands measures more than 1.8 m (6 ft) above sea level.
17. B) São Paulo, Brazil, with over 21 million people.
18. Ayers Rock
19. They lie directly opposite each other on either side of the Earth.
20. Argentina, Bolivia, Colombia, Guyana, Paraguay, Peru, Suriname, Uruguay, Venezuela and France (in the form of French Guiana, an overseas department of France). Only Chile and Ecuador do not share a border with Brazil.

Quiz 3
1. C) 21,196 km (13,170 miles)
2. The All Blacks
3. The Tall Blacks (geddit?)
4. A) Tropic of Cancer
5. A) El Dorado
6. Hungary
7. A) Charles Lindbergh. The feat turned the American aviator into a global celebrity.
8. Calvados
9. Mountain gorillas
10. B) Croatia
11. Neil Armstrong and Edwin 'Buzz' Aldrin
12. Swahili

13. France. TGV stands for '*Train à Grande Vitesse*' ('High-Speed Train').
14. B) California, with approximately 39.5 million people.
15. Rio de Janeiro
16. Sarajevo (in what is now Bosnia and Hercegovina).
17. Noah's Ark
18. C) 2001, on 1 January
19. The Colosseum
20. Maine, Maryland, Massachusetts, Michigan, Minnesota, Mississippi, Missouri and Montana

Quiz 4
Capital Cities
1. Beijing, China
2. Paris, France
3. Washington DC, USA
4. Moscow, Russia
5. Buenos Aires, Argentina
6. Berlin, Germany
7. Tokyo, Japan
8. Wellington, New Zealand
9. Dublin, Ireland
10. Kuala Lumpur, Malaysia
11. Athens, Greece
12. Amsterdam, Netherlands
13. Havana, Cuba
14. Copenhagen, Denmark
15. Mexico City, Mexico
16. Prague, Czech Republic
17. Cape Town, South Africa (note, Cape Town is one of three South African capitals: Cape Town is the legislative capital, Pretoria is the administrative capital, while Bloemfontein is the judicial capital).
18. Lisbon, Portugal
19. Cairo, Egypt
20. Canberra, Australia

Answers

Quiz 5

1. Cabbage
2. Australia
3. Asia
4. Mt St Helens
5. C) A South American horseman
6. The Suez Canal
7. Edinburgh. It's the Edinburgh Festival Fringe.
8. C) Hong Kong. At the last count (and these things change fast), Hong Kong had 317 skyscrapers compared to New York's 257 and Dubai's 177.
9. A) Dried, cured meat, usually served in strips.
10. B) Eight
11. B) Thailand
12. Kellogg. The cereals they invented are still sold all over the world.
13. *The Scream*
14. Sydney Opera House
15. Sporran
16. C) Real
17. A bat, specifically a fruit bat. They are the world's largest species of bat with some individuals growing up to 1.5 m (4ft 11 in) long (or around about the size of a fox).
18. Barack Obama, who was born in Hawaii.
19. The Sun King ('Roi Soleil')
20. African elephant, black rhinoceros, lion, leopard and Cape buffalo

Quiz 6

1. Vegemite
2. B) Marseille with a population of 862,000. Lyon is third with 513,000 and Toulouse fourth with 472,000.
3. Rio de Janeiro
4. A) Mexico, at Chichén Itzá.
5. B) Neptune, which lies beyond Uranus, the second furthest, around 4.495 billion km (2.79 billion miles) from the Sun. Pluto, which lies further out, is now considered a dwarf planet rather than a full planet.
6. The Sistine Chapel, part of the Pope's official residence in the Vatican City, Rome. And you'd have to look up, as it's on the ceiling. The great painter decorated the entire ceiling with biblically themed paintings between 1508 and 1512.
7. A) Morocco
8. B) 71%
9. The Indian Ocean
10. Fidel Castro
11. Holi
12. Jason. His boat was called the *Argo*.
13. Robben Island. It lies in Table Bay to the west of Cape Town.
14. C) South America. It lies at the continent's southern tip.
15. 'Advance Australia Fair'
16. Ghee
17. The Tiber
18. Seal
19. Six
20. Clockwise from north: Mongolia, Russia, North Korea, Vietnam, Laos, Myanmar, India, Bhutan, Nepal, Pakistan, Afghanistan, Tajikistan, Kyrgyzstan and Kazakhstan

Quiz 7

1. The Indian Ocean
2. Seoul
3. C) The Arctic Circle. It's the polar bear.
4. Lego
5. Sake
6. B) Turkey. Although closely associated with the Netherlands, the first tulips didn't arrive there until the 16th century, where they soon became hugely popular. Today, the Netherlands leads the world in tulip cultivation.
7. Mt Kilimanjaro in Tanzania.
8. B) American football
9. The Amazon
10. Tasmania
11. Spain
12. USA. Puerto Ricans are American citizens, although, as the country isn't a state, they cannot vote in the presidential elections or elect members of Congress.
13. France
14. *Santa María*
15. B) 1789
16. C) Kenya
17. Tower Bridge, London, UK
18. B) Detroit
19. C) Japan
20. New Hampshire, New Jersey, New Mexico and New York

Answers

Quiz 8
Food and Drink

1. B) An oven, traditionally made of clay.
2. A) Bourbon
3. Australia and New Zealand
4. Guinea pig
5. Greece
6. Seaweed
7. Louisiana
8. A) Yorkshire
9. Nutmeg
10. Moussaka
11. Yoghurt
12. B) A glass of beer
13. Avocados
14. B) Belgium
15. Caviar – which is the roe, or eggs, of the fish.
16. Filo
17. Italy
18. C) 45 million
19. B) Fufu
20. B) USA. Despite being named after a Mexican state, the sauce was invented in the US, where it has been produced in Louisiana since 1868.

Quiz 9

1. New York
2. A) The Land of the Long White Cloud
3. Rio de Janeiro
4. Hamburg
5. In the USA, along parts of the west coast in the states of California and Oregon.
6. Dim sum
7. Mexico. It's named after the Mexican state of the same name.
8. *Sputnik 1*
9. Africa
10. Toronto
11. Hadrian's Wall. It was named after the emperor who ordered its construction.
12. C) Tokyo, Japan, ahead of Mexico City in second place and Sydney in third.
13. Père Lachaise
14. The jaguar
15. C) 1950s. 1959, to be exact.
16. Loire
17. C) South Sudan
18. The Great Wall of China
19. Sherlock Holmes
20. Afghanistan, Pakistan, India, Nepal, Bhutan and China

Quiz 10

1. Etna on Sicily
2. 'Waltzing Matilda'
3. Ice hockey. It's awarded to the NHL (National Hockey League) play-off winner.
4. South America. It's a llama crossing warning sign, common in Peru, Chile, Bolivia and other Andean countries.
5. B) Apollo 11. Apollo 8 was the first mission to reach the Moon, although it didn't touch down on the surface. Apollo 17 in 1972 was the last mission to put humans on the Moon.
6. C) 90%
7. B) Forest – the Amazon rainforest, in fact.
8. A) New York
9. B) A sausage
10. San Francisco
11. A dragon
12. Rome. They link two of the city's squares.
13. A) South Africa. Weighing 3106.75 carats (621.35 g), it was split into nine smaller stones that went on to adorn the British crown jewels.
14. Poutine
15. C) Santiago
16. Australia
17. The Great Sphinx. The head is supposedly based on the pharaoh Khafre whose pyramid stands nearby.
18. Nepal. It's in the town of Lukla near Mt Everest Base Camp and is mainly used by people aiming to climb the mountain.
19. The USA. The desert lies in the southwest, mainly in California and Nevada.
20. The eight winners are Uruguay, Italy, Germany (including West Germany), Brazil, England, Argentina, France and Spain. Brazil is the only country to have won the tournament five times.

Quiz 11
Sports Venues

1. C) Chicago Cubs
2. C) Russia
3. B) The French Open
4. B) Glasgow
5. A) The Kentucky Derby
6. B) Estadio Azteca
7. B) Cricket
8. C) Old Trafford
9. A) Toronto Maple Leafs
10. B) The Bird's Nest
11. C) Los Angeles
12. A) Parc des Princes
13. C) The US Open
14. B) India. It's named after the country's first prime minister.
15. C) St Andrews
16. C) Las Vegas
17. A) Australia. It's the nickname of the Brisbane Cricket Ground.
18. B) 1995

Answers

19. C) Argentina

20. B) Oakland

21. A) London

22. B) Formula One motor racing

23. A) Barcelona

24. C) USA and Europe

25. A) Madison Square Garden

Quiz 12

1. France

2. B) Russia

3. Antarctica

4. Machu Picchu

5. Diwali

6. South Africa

7. C) New Zealand

8. Brazil

9. A) Ottawa

10. Munich

11. *Crocodile Dundee* in 1986.

12. Just two: Canada and Mexico.

13. Denmark

14. El Salvador

15. The Red Sea

16. Amsterdam

17. Elvis Presley

18. A) Sydney, Australia

19. B) Lord Horatio Nelson, the British naval hero, who was shot and killed during Britain's victory over the French at the Battle of Trafalgar in 1805.

20. The 12 signs are, in order: Rat, Ox, Tiger, Rabbit, Dragon, Snake, Horse, Goat, Monkey, Rooster, Dog and Pig

Quiz 13

1. China. It's held on the 15th day of the traditional Chinese New Year celebrations.

2. C) Ulaanbaatar

3. The kiwi

4. The Valley of the Kings

5. C) Russia

6. Singapore Sling

7. Romania

8. True. They're also known as grolar bears and nanulaks and are found in parts of northern Canada.

9. A geyser. It erupts every 44 to 125 minutes, shooting boiling water up to a height of 56 m (185 ft).

10. Italy

11. C) A type of drum, traditionally made of goatskin and hardwood.

12. Portuguese

13. New Orleans

14. South America. It's also known as the Andean bear.

15. C) USA and UK

16. Berlin is first with around 3.6 million people, followed by Rome with 2.9 million and then Paris with 2.2 million.

17. Melbourne, Australia – MCG stands for the Melbourne Cricket Ground. Seating over 100,000 spectators, it's the world's largest cricket ground.

18. Germany – although a top speed of 130 kph (80 mph) is 'recommended'.

19. Times Square

20. 1. Mandarin Chinese, 2. Spanish, 3. English, 4. Arabic, 5. Hindi, 6. Bengali, 7. Portuguese, 8. Russian, 9. Japanese, 10. Punjabi

Quiz 14

1. A) The Louvre with 9 million visitors a year; the National Museum of Natural History is second with 8 million; while the National Museum of China is third with 7.5 million.

2. Nevada

3. Have a drink. It's a caffeine-rich beverage made with dried leaves of the yerba mate plant.

4. The British monarch, currently Queen Elizabeth II, who remains the head of state of both nations (as well as another 14 nations, including Canada).

5. Gazpacho

6. Chicago

7. Komodo. It's the Komodo dragon, which can grow up to 3 m (10 ft long).

8. C) Buenos Aires

9. England, Scotland, Wales and Northern Ireland

10. The Mounties

11. Venice

12. 26 January. It marks the arrival of the fleet of British ships in 1788 and the establishment of the settlement that would become Sydney.

13. Florida

14. A) A circular tent, traditionally made from animal skins and used by the nomadic peoples of Central Asia.

15. Lake Victoria

16. B) Sweden

17. Durian

18. B) The American flag, also known as the Stars and Stripes.

19. Rum and cola

20. 1. US dollar, 2. Euro, 3. Japanese yen, 4. Pound sterling, 5. Australian dollar,

Answers

6. Canadian dollar, 7. Swiss franc,
8. Chinese renminbi (Yuan),
9. Swedish krona,
10. New Zealand dollar

Quiz 15
Guess the City

1. Las Vegas, USA
2. Rio de Janeiro, Brazil
3. Copenhagen, Denmark
4. Cairo, Egypt
5. Istanbul, Turkey
6. Sydney, Australia
7. Montreal, Canada
8. Buenos Aires, Argentina
9. Edinburgh, Scotland
10. Tokyo, Japan
11. Moscow, Russia
12. Kingston, Jamaica

Quiz 16

1. B) A series of giant pictures measuring several hundred metres across, etched in the desert of southern Peru between 500 BCE and 500 CE by the Nazca people. Some are geometric patterns, while others depict animals, including monkeys, spiders and hummingbirds.
2. Australia
3. Empire State Building
4. B) Lager. The name derives from the fact that lagers take around twice as long to brew as ales, and so have to be stored longer.
5. The hook and eye fastener known as Velcro (from the French words *velours* meaning 'velvet' and *crochet* meaning 'hook'). He got the idea from examining how sticky seeds called burrs attached themselves to his clothing using tiny hooks on their surface.

6. St Petersburg, Russia
7. The ostrich
8. Chicago
9. Wind. A revised version of his scale is still used today.
10. The Orient Express. Although timetabled services have ended, a private contractor still runs services bearing the name Orient Express.
11. Portugal
12. China. It's believed that the cultivation of mulberry moths for silk began as far back as 3000 BCE.
13. The Himalayas
14. C) Florida. A concrete obelisk, called the Southernmost Point Buoy, marks the spot in Key West.
15. A dog called Laika (meaning 'barker' in Russian), which was sent up by the Soviet Union in 1957. It didn't survive the journey.
16. Lagos, Nigeria
17. New Zealand
18. The opossum
19. Cannes on the French Riviera. The festival began in 1946.
20. Venezuela, Colombia, Ecuador, Peru, Bolivia, Chile and Argentina

Quiz 17

1. B) Manila
2. The Day of the Dead
3. HMY *Britannia*
4. C) A cake. It's a sponge cake covered in chocolate and coconut, named after Lord Lamington, who served as Governor of Queensland from 1896 to 1901.
5. The Atlantic
6. C) Italy
7. Seattle

8. Turtle
9. A) Cuba
10. Rhode Island
11. Sri Lanka
12. Pelé
13. B) Venice
14. Sir Edmund Hillary, the conqueror of Everest. He also died in Auckland in 2008, aged 88.
15. An elephant
16. The Russian cosmonaut, Yuri Gagarin
17. The Grand Canyon
18. C) Seine
19. A) Poland. It's flavoured with bison grass grown in the country's Białowieża Forest.
20. The Met

Quiz 18

1. Niagara Falls
2. Red and gold/yellow
3. Mexico
4. Amerigo Vespucci (1454– 1512). He was the first person to realise that the Americas were not part of Asia (as Columbus had assumed) but separate continents, then unknown to both Europe and Asia.
5. Tajine
6. The orangutan, which can be found only in Malaysia and Indonesia.
7. A) The Nile... just. Most sources put the Nile first on 6650 km (4132 miles) with the Amazon second on 6400 km (4000 miles), the Yangtze third on 6300 km (3915 miles) and the Mississippi fourth on 6197 km (3870 miles).
8. New Zealand
9. Los Angeles. They are the city's

Answers

American football (Chargers), basketball (Lakers) and soccer (Galaxy) teams.
10. C) Zebra
11. Oranges
12. Smallville
13. The rupee
14. The Thames
15. C) A Sydneysider
16. The Black Death
17. C) Venice. It shows a gondolier on The Grand Canal.
18. The Pacific Ocean
19. The Louvre, Paris
20. A) Sweden, B) Iceland, C) Jamaica, D) France, E) Israel, F) Canada, G) New Zealand, H) South Korea, I) Barbados, J) Colombia, K) Australia, L) Ireland

Quiz 19 – Wildlife Around the World

1. The cheetah, which in short bursts can hit top speeds of up to 120 kph (75 mph).
2. C) Emperor
3. C) The peregrine falcon, which can reach speeds of over 300 kph (186 mph) when diving for prey. The swift is the fastest bird in level flight, reaching top speeds of 112 kph (70 mph), while the ostrich is the fastest bird on two legs, capable of running at 70 kph (44 mph).
4. B) The giant squid. Its eyes can measure up to 27 cm (10.6 in) across, the size of a dinner plate.
5. A) They're the only mammals that lay eggs rather than giving birth to live young.
6. C) It's a large, venomous tree snake from sub-Saharan Africa.

7. Reindeer
8. Panda
9. Piranha
10. The Galápagos
11. C) Dingo
12. A) Crustaceans – they look a bit like tiny shrimp.
13. Chameleons
14. Cougar
15. A) They build the largest nests of any birds, which can house over 100 pairs.
16. A) Gibraltar. Around two hundred Barbary macaques, the descendants of a population that was introduced several centuries ago, make the rock their home.
17. A fish
18. C) Exactly the same as a human: seven. They're just much bigger.
19. Sea cow
20. A) Blue. Octopus blood is copper-based, rather than iron-based like mammal blood, giving it a blue hue.

Quiz 20

1. Hyena
2. The Alps. France and Italy.
3. C) Minneapolis
4. The Loch Ness Monster. The image was later revealed to be a fake made using a toy submarine and clay.
5. Australia
6. The footprints, handprints and signatures of famous movie stars from the 1920s to the present day, which have been embedded in concrete blocks.
7. South Korea
8. Barcelona. Antoni Gaudí.
9. Denim (from 'de Nîmes', meaning 'of Nîmes').

10. Rio de Janeiro
11. St Paul's Cathedral
12. Grasses
13. Scotland
14. Tamale
15. Germany
16. Argentina. It's an archipelago at the southern tip of the continent.
17. Mongolia. The Gobi is the world's fourth largest desert.
18. Copenhagen in Denmark and Malmö in Sweden.
19. The San Andreas Fault. Movements of the plates have caused several earthquakes, including the particularly devastating 1906 San Francisco earthquake.
20. New South Wales, Queensland, South Australia, Tasmania, Victoria and Western Australia. The country also has 10 territories (including several islands), the largest of which is the Northern Territory on the Australian mainland.

Quiz 21

1. North Korea
2. C) White
3. Broadway
4. London
5. South Africa
6. B) Russia
7. Venice
8. C) Rabbits. Introduced by the first European settlers in the late 18th century, by the early 20th century rabbits had become a major pest – and remain so to this day.
9. Boats or ships
10. Chicago
11. Algeria

Answers

12. Amsterdam, the Netherlands

13. Mexico – the biggest celebrations actually take place in the US rather than Mexico.

14. A) Tokyo is first with around 9.6 million, followed by B) Mexico City with around 8.9 million and then C) New York: with around 8.6 million.

15. C) Chile

16. B) Guangzhou

17. Bagheera

18. B) The goliath bird-eater – with a leg span of around 28 cm (11 in), it's the largest known spider in terms of body size.

19. Mt Rushmore

20. A) Switzerland

Quiz 22
Country Club

1. A) Canada

2. B) Cuba

3. C) Colombia

4. A) Argentina

5. B) Iceland

6. B) Ireland

7. B) Sweden

8. C) Germany

9. A) Portugal

10. B) Morocco

11. C) Egypt

12. C) Kenya

13. A) South Africa

14. B) Madagascar

15. C) India

16. A) Mongolia

17. B) Thailand

18. C) Japan

19. A) Papua New Guinea

20. B) New Zealand

Quiz 23

1. Canada

2. Deer

3. B) Yellow

4. New York

5. Australia. The Great Barrier Reef is the world's largest structure built by living organisms. It's so big it can be seen from outer space.

6. C) Louvre, Paris

7. C) Tiger. The peacock is the national bird and the lion was the national animal until being replaced by the tiger in 1972.

8. The Netherlands

9. C) Charles Bridge

10. B) Ethiopia

11. The *Bounty*

12. Galileo Galilei

13. Whirling Dervishes

14. Boston and Florence

15. It's the appropriately named whale shark, which can grow up to 9.8 m (32 ft) long and weigh 9 tonnes (20,000 lb).

16. B) The Southern Cross

17. Stalin, the leader of the Soviet Union from the mid-1920s to 1953. 'Stalin' means 'Man of Steel' in Russian.

18. Florence

19. India

20. Brazil, Bolivia, Peru, Ecuador, Colombia, Venezuela, Guyana, Suriname and France (in the form of French Guiana)

Quiz 24

1. It's Rome, strange as it may seem, which has a latitude of 41.90°N, compared to 40.73°N for New York.

2. Madagascar

3. Noah's Ark

4. B) Amazon

5. A spicy stew (or soup) served over rice, from Louisiana, USA.

6. It's probably a smaller one than you might think – the mosquito. Mosquito-transmitted malaria kills on average over 500,000 people a year in sub-Saharan Africa.

7. Not the lion or the elephant, both of which cause few deaths, but the hippopotamus. Extremely aggressive, with large powerful teeth, it kills around 500 people in Africa each year.

8. Venice

9. Museum of Modern Art

10. B) Singapore is first with around 5.6 million people, followed by Sydney with 4.3 million and Kuala Lumpur with 1.3 million.

11. B) The red kangaroo

12. San Francisco

13. A) India

14. Atlas Mountains

15. Machu Picchu

16. Barcelona and Real Madrid

17. Malta

18. B) 20%

19. Beatrix Potter

20. England and South Africa

Answers

Quiz 25

1. Glastonbury
2. New Zealand
3. Tiger
4. Russia
5. B) Africa
6. Switzerland
7. Havana
8. Sami
9. Spanish
10. B) Bark
11. C) New York
12. A) Egypt
13. B) James Bond Island
14. Rome
15. Red, white and blue
16. C) Canadian dollar
17. C) Canberra
18. B) The Irish Sea
19. Andalucía
20. B) New Zealand

Quiz 26

1. C) Australia. There have been no recorded eruptions since the arrival of the first European settlers in the late 18th century.
2. B) New York, USA
3. C) Rice balls, often filled with meat sauce and/or cheese. Covered in breadcrumbs, they're fried, turning them a deep orange colour, which gives them their name, meaning 'little oranges'.
4. B) Ecuador
5. A) Mecca
6. B) African elephant
7. C) St Lawrence
8. Chile
9. B) 4. The superstition is believed to have arisen because the Chinese words for 'four' and 'death' sound almost identical.

10. Anzac Day (it's named after the Australian and New Zealand Army Corps – ANZAC).
11. Kiev
12. A) France, at roughly 640,000 sq km (247,400 sq miles), followed by B) Spain at 506,000 sq km (195,400 sq miles) and then C) Germany at 357,400 sq km (138,000 square miles).
13. A) The Roman goddess of love
14. C) Ethiopia
15. Japan
16. B) UK
17. Christchurch
18. B) Buddhism
19. The Dead Sea – its high salt content makes people more buoyant than they are in normal salty or fresh water.
20. Norway, Sweden, Denmark, Finland and Iceland

Quiz 27
Silhouette Cities

1. A) London
2. B) Toronto
3. B) Sydney
4. C) Dubai
5. C) New York
6. B) Paris
7. A) Kuala Lumpur
8. C) Tokyo
9. B) Moscow
10. A) Cairo
11. B) Rio de Janeiro
12. C) Barcelona

Quiz 28

1. B) Michelin
2. Hajj
3. Sydney
4. Sushi
5. Milan
6. Africa
7. The World Series
8. The Gherkin
9. C) The lira
10. Mediterranean Sea
11. Almonds (specifically ground almonds)
12. C) Argentina is the largest at roughly 2.78 million sq km (1.07 million sq miles) followed by B) Peru with 1.3 million sq km (496,000 sq miles) and A) Chile with 756,000 sq km (292,000 sq miles).
13. Provence
14. The Twelve Apostles
15. B) Caribbean Sea
16. B) Colombia
17. B) French
18. A) Black Sea
19. Stonehenge
20. A) British Empire. At its peak in the 1920s (shortly before it began to dissolve), it covered more than a fifth of the Earth's land mass and 20% of its people. The Mongol Empire, which reached its peak in the 13th century, was the largest contiguous empire in history, covering 24 million sq km (9.2 million sq miles) of Asia.

Quiz 29

1. Silicon Valley
2. B) South Africa
3. B) A round flatbread
4. C) Australia. It was built to keep dingoes out of the fertile southeast of the continent and was largely successful.
5. B) Red Sea
6. Seattle, USA to Sydney, Australia
7. The Berlin Wall
8. A) Men
9. A) Venus
10. C) Turkey
11. Millennium Dome
12. Argentina. His second wife Eva Perón was the subject of a long running Andrew Lloyd Webber musical, *Evita*.
13. C) New Zealand
14. A) Mississippi
15. B) Mexico
16. A) Lisbon
17. Ganges
18. B) Japan
19. Australia. Technically Oceania, the wider area featured in many atlases, isn't a continent (a single land mass) but a continental grouping used to include places that aren't part of the Australian land mass, such as New Zealand and Polynesia.
20. A) Ravens. At least six ravens are kept at the tower at any one time – with their wings clipped just in case they get any ideas about moving on.

Quiz 30

1. On the Moon. They're the names of two lunar maria (plains caused by volcanic activity).
2. C) Amazon, Brazil
3. B) Mexico
4. A) Coca-Cola. Back then it was a much more potent concoction, originally containing both caffeine and cocaine.
5. C) A folded pizza
6. A) Canada. With its many lakes, Canada has a total surface area of water of 891,163 sq km (344,080 sq miles).
7. Vienna, Austria
8. Cairo has around 9.2 million people compared to 7.9 million in Johannesburg.
9. A) Australia
10. A) Grilled meats
11. The Shard
12. Libya
13. C) Honduras – it's in Central America.
14. The Pacific Ocean
15. A) Saudi Arabia with roughly 2.15 million sq km (830,000 sq miles), followed by B) Iran with 1.6 million sq km (640,000 sq miles) and C) Egypt with 1.01 million sq km (390,000 sq miles).
16. C) Egypt with roughly 98 million people, followed by B) Iran with 81 million and A) Saudi Arabia with 33 million.
17. London
18. Tasmania
19. William Shakespeare. It's the Globe, a modern replica of the Elizabethan theatre where he premiered many of his plays.
20. The colours are, from left to right: blue, yellow, black, green and red.

Chapter 2
Traveller (Medium)

Quiz 31 General Knowledge

1. The 20 busiest railway stations can all be found in which country?

2. What type of animal was Lonesome George, the last of his species, who died in 2012 on the Galápagos Islands?

3. The Jorvik Viking Centre is located in which English city?
A) Leeds B) Liverpool C) York

4. Produced by the world's oldest rum distillery, established in 1703, Mount Gay Rum is made on which Caribbean island?

5. In what country is the Gir Forest, home to the only wild lions found outside Africa?

6. What common food item, now eaten across the world, was named after the British aristocrat John Montagu in the 18th century?

7. What New Zealand actor starred as Dr Alan Grant in the first *Jurassic Park* film in 1993?

8. What museum would you need to visit if you wanted to take a look at Vincent Van Gogh's *The Starry Night*?
A) National Gallery, London
B) Museum of Modern Art, New York
C) Rijksmuseum, Amsterdam

9. What river flows through the Russian capital, Moscow?

10. Grappa is a type of grape-based brandy from which country?

11. What is the national animal of Canada?
A) Beaver B) Moose C) Kangaroo

12. The *Colombina*, the *Volto* and the *Medico della Pesta* ('Plague Doctor') are all types of what, often worn at the Venice Carnival?

13. What famous tourist attraction opened on 17 July 1955, in Anaheim, California?
A) Disneyland B) Disney World
C) Bush Gardens

14. A Unesco World Heritage Site, the Great Mosque of Djenné is in which African country?
A) Mali B) South Africa C) Nigeria

15. Served in curries in parts of India, what sort of creature is a Bombay duck?
A) A bird B) A fish C) An octopus

16. In what country is the opera *Aida* set? And, for a bonus point, who wrote it?

17. The Chinese administrative region of Macau was officially controlled by which country between 1887 and 1999?
A) Britain B) Spain C) Portugal

18. What is the name of the caramelised spread made by heating sweetened milk that is popular in Latin America?

19. What sort of animal is a bilby?
A) A bird B) A fish C) A marsupial

20. What is the name of this party street, which runs through the US city often described as the 'Entertainment Capital of the World'?

© f1lphoto / Shutterstock

Quiz 32 **General Knowledge**

1. Which city is furthest north?
A) Vancouver, Canada
B) Edinburgh, Scotland
C) Moscow, Russia

2. On 3 April, 1973, at the Hilton Hotel, New York, a Motorola engineer called Martin Cooper, become the first person to do what?
A) Make a mobile phone call
B) Send a text message
C) Log on to the internet

3. Which building in Jerusalem is believed by Muslims to be where the prophet Muhammad ascended to heaven?

4. Now performed by New Zealand sports teams at the start of a match, the Māori haka was traditionally staged before what?

5. What object, discovered by French soldiers in 1799, finally allowed scholars to decipher ancient Egyptian hieroglyphs?

6. He's most closely associated with the Cuban Revolution, but in what country was Che Guevara born? And, for a couple of bonus points, in what country was he killed, and in what year?

7. Plains, mountain and Grévy's are species of what African mammal?

8. In 2015, the name of America's tallest mountain was changed from Mt McKinley to what?

9. Edmund Barton served as the first prime minister of which country from 1901 to 1903?
A) Canada B) Australia C) UK

10. In the Caribbean, a 'duppy' is a word for a what?
A) A type of pastry B) A sailing boat
C) A ghost

11. What iconic 20th-century music venue was designed by the Danish architect Jørn Utzon? Clue: it was completed in 1973 and it's a long way from Denmark.

12. Found living at a depth of 7,966 m (26,135 ft) in the Mariana Trench, making it the deepest-living creature yet found, *Pseudoliparis swirei* is what sort of animal?
A) A fish B) A crab C) A worm

13. In 1841, a British cabinetmaker organised a 12-mile train journey so five hundred people could attend a temperance meeting. The trip was such a success that it prompted him to found a successful holiday business. What was the cabinetmaker's name?

14. What is the Welsh word for Wales?

15. Minsk is the capital of which country?
A) Ukraine B) Belarus C) Mexico

16. What does the large stone tower in London known simply as 'The Monument' commemorate?
A) The signing of Magna Carta in 1215
B) The Peasants' Revolt of 1381
C) The Great Fire of London in 1666

17. What is Asia's largest desert?

18. Which country has the most extensive rail network in the world?
A) China B) USA C) Spain

19. What five-letter Danish word is used to describe a feeling of cosy contentment and well-being?

20. Can you name the five African countries that have coastlines on the Mediterranean Sea? You get a point for each.

Answers on p.96   Score

Quiz 33 **General Knowledge**

1. Which Russian mountain range conventionally marks the boundary between Europe and Asia?

2. The island of Hispaniola, on which the first permanent European settlement in the Americas was founded, is now shared by which two countries?

3. What is the only South American country to boast both an Atlantic and a Pacific coast?

4. Vientiane is the capital of which country?

5. Which Central American country, a major ecotourism destination, is sandwiched between Panama to the south and Nicaragua to the north?

6. Switzerland has three nationwide official languages. What are they?

7. What is the northernmost country in Africa?

8. The largest living organism on Earth is found in the Blue Mountains of the US state of Oregon. What is it?
A) A tree **B)** A fungus **C)** A moss

9. In what city was the composer Wolfgang Amadeus Mozart born?
A) Vienna **B)** Salzburg **C)** Paris

10. A type of critically endangered amphibian, the axolotl is a salamander native to just two lakes in which country?
A) Mexico **B)** Australia **C)** UK

11. What are the only two landlocked countries in South America?

12. The Seikan Tunnel connects islands in which country?

13. The world's largest statue (as of 2018) is in which country?
A) USA **B)** China **C)** India

14. Reigning from 37 to 41 CE, the Roman emperor Gaius Julius Caesar Augustus Germanicus is better known by what name, meaning 'Little Boots'?

15. What are the names of the two small countries that lie completely enclosed within the borders of Italy?

16. The British naturalist Jane Goodall spent over 50 years in Tanzania studying which primates?

17. Kigali is the capital of which African country?
A) Angola **B)** Zimbabwe **C)** Rwanda

18. The pampas is a region of flat treeless plains in what continent?

19. '*La Serenissima*' (meaning 'most serene') and 'Queen of the Adriatic' are among the nicknames of which Italian city?

20. Name this famous European landmark?

© Nuaehnaja / Shutterstock

Answers on p.96   Score ☐

Quiz 34 **Mountains**

1. In what year did the New Zealander Sir Edmund Hillary and the Nepalese Tenzing Norgay become the first people to reach the summit of Mt Everest, the world's tallest mountain?

2. Just how tall is Mt Everest?
A) 6848 m (22, 467 ft)
B) 8848 m (29,029 ft)
C) 10,048 m (32,966 ft)

3. What is the second highest mountain on Earth?

4. If the oceans were drained of all their water, what then would be the highest mountain on Earth?

5. If Russia is considered European, what is the highest mountain in Europe?

6. And what is Europe's highest peak outside of Russia?

7. Mt Vinson is the highest mountain on which continent?

8. What is the highest mountain in the USA outside Alaska?
A) Mt Massive B) Mt Whitney
C) Mt Rushmore

9. Mt Toubkal is the highest mountain in which range? And, for a bonus point, what country is it in?

10. Moving beyond Earth, what and where is the tallest mountain in the entire solar system?

11. What is the longest mountain range on Earth (excluding undersea ranges)?

12. The Pyrenees mountain range forms a natural border between which two countries?

13. Which mountain range in northeast Italy shares its name with the mineral calcium magnesium carbonate?

14. Kibo, Mawenzi and Shira are the three dormant cones atop which African volcanic mountain?

15. On 30 April 1985, Richard Bass became the first person to achieve what extreme mountaineering feat?
A) Climbing Mt Everest backwards
B) Climbing the highest peak on all seven continents
C) Climbing the Andes lengthways

16. In 1885, Edward Whymper led the expedition that conquered which Alpine peak, then considered one of the most dangerous in the world?

17. Which mountain was supposedly the home of the ancient Greek gods?

18. Georgia and Azerbaijan are separated from Russia by which mountain range, which also gives its name to the wider region?

19. What name is given to Scottish mountains over 3000 ft (914 m) high?
A) Bunros
B) Funros
C) Munros

20. What and where is the highest mountain outside of Asia? And, for a bonus point, where does it rank in the list of highest mountains?
A) 9th
B) 29th
C) 189th

Answers on p.97   Score

Quiz 35 **General Knowledge**

1. What is the world's most southerly capital city?
A) Cape Town, South Africa
B) Wellington, New Zealand
C) Buenos Aires, Argentina

2. And, by way of contrast, what is the world's most northerly capital city?
A) Ottawa, Canada
B) Helsinki, Finland
C) Reykjavík, Iceland

3. The Declaration of Independence, the document that kick-started the American War of Independence, was signed on 4 July 1776, in which US city?
A) Washington DC
B) Philadelphia
C) New York

4. According to the 1897 novel, *Dracula*, in what Yorkshire coastal resort did the vampiric count first set foot in Britain?

5. What two South American countries share the region of Patagonia?

6. Played in four separate countries (on three different continents), what are the four grand slam (or major) tennis tournaments?

7. Every year in Lopburi, Thailand, the local people put on a festival to honour (and provide food for) what type of animal?

8. What three countries have coastlines on both the Mediterranean Sea and the Atlantic Ocean?

9. Who founded the Egyptian city of Alexandria, and, for a bonus point, in what century?

10. Which South American country is named after an Italian city?

11. How is the 243 km (151 mile) stretch of road along the southern coast of Victoria, Australia, more commonly known?

12. What famous family of writers lived at a parsonage in Haworth, Yorkshire, England, now a major tourist attraction?

13. The 1961 Bay of Pigs Invasion was a failed attempt to overthrow the government of which country?

14. What is the name of the Japanese martial art practised with bamboo swords?
A) Aikido B) Ikebana C) Kendo

15. Located in Everett, Washington, USA, with a volume of over 13 million cubic metres (427 million cubic feet), the world's largest building is a factory operated by which company?
A) Microsoft B) Amazon C) Boeing

16. Alnwick Castle in Northumberland, England, was used for the exterior shots of what in a series of blockbuster films beginning in 2001?

17. In which state is the Augusta National Golf Club, the venue for the US Masters golf championship?

18. What country has the longest coastline?
A) Canada B) Russia C) Australia

19. The tallest statue in Africa is located in what city?
A) Dakar, Senegal
B) Cairo, Egypt
C) Nairobi, Kenya

20. What is the only city to have hosted the Summer Olympics three times? And, for three bonus points, can you name the years?

Quiz 36 **General Knowledge**

1. Which country has the greatest number of volcanoes?
A) USA B) Russia C) Indonesia

2. What South American country is named after a line of latitude?

3. What event was the Eiffel Tower built to commemorate?

4. Beginning with 'G', what is the smallest mainland country in Africa by area?

5. What two countries are linked by the Khyber Pass?

6. What Australian city is this?
A) Gold Coast B) Darwin C) Perth

7. What planet was discovered by the German-British astronomer Sir William Herschel in 1781?
A) Saturn B) Uranus C) Neptune

8. With 158 verses, which country has the longest national anthem?
A) Vanuatu B) Belize C) Greece

9. The film *The Third Man* is set in which European city?

10. The Brazilian footballer Pelé famously described soccer as '*o jogo bonito*'. What does '*o jogo bonito*' mean?
A) Jogging with a ball B) The beautiful game
C) Goal bonanza

11. Nathan's Diner in New York City hosts a competition every 4 July in which people try to speed eat what fast-food item?
A) Boiled eggs B) Hot dogs C) Kebabs

12. Hannibal, the general who marched his elephants across the Alps to confront the Romans during the Punic Wars, was from which North African city state?

13. Gruyère cheese comes from which European country?

14. Why was the 1969 film *Krakatoa, East of Java* renamed *Volcano* in the 1970s?
A) Market research suggested that films with single-word titles did better than those with multi-word titles
B) Audiences found the word 'Krakatoa' difficult to pronounce
C) Krakatoa is actually west of Java

15. What European city does the River Liffey flow through?

16. In 1946, the French fashion designer Louis Réard introduced the bikini, named after Bikini Atoll in the Pacific Ocean, which had recently been in the news for what reason?

17. Leinster House, the seat of the Irish parliament in Dublin, provided the inspiration for which famous US building?

18. What is the name of the lake that occupies mainland Australia's lowest point? In wet periods, it is the country's largest lake but in dry periods has very little water in it.

19. A five-time winner of the Formula One World Championship, Juan Manuel Fangio was a racing driver from which country?

20. What three US states have just four letters in their name? You get a point for each.

Answers on p.97 Score

Quiz 37 **General Knowledge**

1. What European country does Tokay (or Tokaji) wine come from?
A) Germany B) Hungary C) Greece

2. Mexico is bordered by the United States and which two Central American countries?
A) Guatemala and Belize
A) Belize and El Salvador
A) El Salvador and Honduras

3. Abuja replaced what city as the capital of Nigeria in 1991?

4. What is the only South American country that has English as an official language?

5. What is Thailand's currency?
A) Baht B) Caht C) Daht

6. The Statue of Liberty holds a torch in her right hand, but what does she hold in her left hand?
A) A writing tablet B) A sword C) A gun

7. Based in the Czech Republic, what car company manufactures models including the Fabia and the Octavia?

8. How many emirates make up the United Arab Emirates?
A) Three B) Seven C) Ten

9. What is the third most common gas in Earth's atmosphere, accounting for around 0.93% of the total?

10. The Hotel Sidi Driss in Matmata, Tunisia, was a used as a set in which series of blockbuster films?

11. The Grand Canyon was carved out of the rock over millions of years by which river?

12. What is the national bird of Australia?
A) Kookaburra B) Cassowary C) Emu

13. What is the UK's largest river by volume?
A) The Thames B) The Severn C) The Tay

14. The flag of which country is composed of red and white horizontal bands with a picture of a green cedar tree at its centre?
A) Laos B) Lebanon C) Lithuania

15. What is the largest city in Switzerland, by population?
A) Zurich B) Basel C) Geneva

16. The annual Coachella music festival is staged at the Empire Polo Club in which US state?
A) Nevada B) Oregon C) California

17. During the communist era, East Germany's State Security Service was commonly known by what shorter name?
A) The KGB B) The Stasi C) The SS

18. Which country is the world's largest exporter of iron ore?
A) Brazil B) Australia C) South Africa

19. The Patio de los Leones (Patio of the Lions), seen here, is part of which enormous Moorish palace complex in the Spanish city of Granada?

© Cezary Wojtkowski / Lonely Planet

20. Russia has land borders with 14 countries. Can you name them? You get a point for each.

Quiz 38 **Currencies and Money**

1. You're strolling the streets of Caracas with a wad of bolívar notes in your pocket, speaking Spanish. Where are you?

2. In what European country could you exchange 100 groszy for 1 złoty?

3. Albania's currency is named after which major figure from ancient history?
A) Julius Caesar
B) Alexander the Great
C) Ramses II
And, for a bonus point, what is the currency called?

4. Costa Rica's currency is named after which famous explorer?
A) Ferdinand Magellan
B) Amerigo Vespucci
C) Christopher Columbus
And, for a bonus point, what is the currency called?

5. From around 600 to 200 BCE, where would it have been possible to pay for things using bronze knives?
A) China B) Turkey C) Egypt

6. According to the ancient Greek historian, Herodotus, the first coins were minted in Lydia. In what modern country was the kingdom of Lydia?
A) China B) Turkey C) Egypt

7. Use of deerskin as a form of barter in 18th-century America gave rise to which slang term for a dollar?

8. During the 17th century, how were Spanish dollars better known in pirate circles?

9. The rand is the currency of which country?

10. In what country was paper money invented, and in what century?

11. What's the highest denomination US dollar bill ever printed?
A) $10,000 B) $100,000 C) $1 million

12. The world's first automatic cash dispenser was installed in 1967 in which city?
A) London B) New York C) Singapore

13. The largest recorded form of currency is the Rai, consisting of giant disc-shaped stones with a hole in the middle. Weighing up to 4 tonnes, they were used as money on the island of Yap. Where is Yap?

14. The world's oldest commercial bank was founded in which country?
A) England B) Sweden C) Germany

15. And the world's oldest central (or state) bank was founded in which country?
A) England B) Sweden C) Germany

16. The pula is the currency of which country?
A) Croatia B) Brazil C) Botswana

17. The Italian artist Arturo di Modica is responsible for a famous animal-themed statue in which financial district?
A) Milan, Italy B) Canary Wharf, London, UK
C) Wall Street, New York, USA

18. What is the currency of Japan?

19. From 1923 to 1924, Germany endured rampant hyperinflation. What was the face value of the highest denomination banknote printed at this time?
A) 1 million B) 100 million C) 100 billion

20. What were these countries' currencies prior to their adoption of the euro? You get a point for each.
A) France B) Germany C) Netherlands
D) Spain E) Italy F) Greece G) Portugal
H) Finland I) Ireland J) Slovenia

Answers on p.98   Score ☐

Quiz 39 **General Knowledge**

1. Published in 1973, what was the name of the first travel guide published by Lonely Planet's co-founders Tony and Maureen Wheeler?
A) *Around Australia in a Van*
B) *Exploring Europe by Train*
C) *Across Asia on the Cheap*

2. The name of which Hawaiian musical instrument translates as 'jumping flea'?

3. According to Chinese legend, Cangjie (c. 2650 BCE), the official historian of the Yellow Emperor, was the inventor of what?
A) Writing B) Music C) Paper

4. In what country would you find the most northerly living wild monkeys?
A) Russia B) Norway C) Japan

5. What country fought a successful war of independence against the Ottoman Empire between 1821 and 1829?
A) Greece B) Egypt C) Saudi Arabia

6. According to legend, through which English city did Lady Godiva ride naked as a protest against the harsh tax regime of her husband, the Count of Mercia? And, for a bonus point, who was the only person to see her do it?

7. The word's largest children's museum is situated in which US city?
A) Miami B) Indianapolis C) Chicago

8. Batmania was one of the former names of which Australian city?

9. In what country would you find the Damnoen Saduak Floating Market?
A) Thailand B) India C) Norway

10. San Salvador is the capital of which Central American country?

11. What is the two-word name for the boundary of a black hole, beyond which nothing can escape its massive gravitational pull?

12. The Tomb of the Unknown Soldier is located beneath which Parisian landmark?
A) Eiffel Tower B) Arc de Triomphe
C) Sacré-Coeur

13. What Greek word, originally meaning 'chief sea', is now used to describe a group of islands?

14. *Pato*, a sort of combination of polo and basketball, is the national sport of which South American country?
A) Chile B) Argentina C) Brazil

15. What was the tallest building in the world for over 3800 years – from around 2560 BCE to around 1311 CE? And, for two bonus points, what succeeded it?

16. Britain's only village with an exclamation mark in its name, Westward Ho!, is in which English county?
A) Devon B) Dorset C) Cornwall

17. What colour helmets do United Nations peacekeeping troops wear?
A) Blue B) White C) Pink

18. In Kenya, what is a matatu?
A) A traditional hat worn at Easter
B) A minibus used as a shared taxi
C) A traditional Masai shield

19. In what country was Marie Antoinette, wife of the French King Louis XVI, born? And, for a bonus point, how did she die?

20. How many of the nine countries that share a land border with Germany can you name? You get a point for each.

Quiz 40 **General Knowledge**

1. What was the name of the British archaeologist who, in 1922, discovered the (mostly) intact tomb of Pharaoh Tutankhamun (c. 1341–1323 BCE) in Egypt?

2. The mountain range known as the Southern Alps are in which country?

3. What's the least populated US state?
A) Wyoming B) Texas C) Alaska

4. The 1964 Olympic Games were held in which Asian city?
A) Beijing B) Tokyo C) Mumbai

5. What is the name of the statue that stands atop Corcovado Mountain overlooking Rio de Janeiro?

6. When Tim Berners-Lee invented the worldwide web he was working for CERN, the European Organization for Nuclear Research. In what city is Cern based?
A) Paris B) Berlin C) Geneva

7. The *sestertius*, the *denarius* and the *as* were denominations of coin used where?

8. In what country does most of the Kalahari Desert lie?
A) Namibia B) Botswana C) Zimbabwe

9. The island group of Murano in the Venice Lagoon is famous for what traditional craft?

10. The Dandy horse and velocipede were early types of which form of transport?

11. Can you name the two great writers, one English, one Spanish, who died on the same day: 23 April 1616?

12. What was the name of the giant glass and iron building constructed for the 1851 Great Exhibition in London?

13. What Australian mammal became extinct in 1936 when the last captive specimen, called Benjamin, died in Australia's Beaumaris Zoo?

14. 'Over the great bridge, with sunlight through the girders making a constant flicker upon the moving cars, with the city rising up across the river in white heaps and sugar lumps… the city seen for the first time, in its first wild promise of all the mystery and the beauty in the world.' What city was F. Scott Fitzgerald describing in this passage from *The Great Gatsby*?

15. Roughly how much of Africa is desert?
A) One third B) One quarter C) One fifth

16. Which South American country is the largest producer of emeralds in the world?
A) Chile B) Colombia C) Bolivia

17. What world wonder was discovered in Xi'an, China, on 29 March 1974, by farmers digging a well?

18. What was the tallest building in the world from 1931 to 1970?

19. What city is this?

A) Shanghai B) Los Angeles C) Singapore

20. Can you list the seven nations whose name ends in 'stan', a Farsi word meaning 'country' or 'place'? You get a point for each.

Answers on p.99   Score

Quiz 41 **General Knowledge**

1. How many stripes are there on the US flag?
A) 13 **B)** 50 **C)** 1776

2. What is the largest lake in England's Lake District?
A) Ullswater **B)** Windermere
C) Coniston Water

3. In which modern country are the ruins of Troy located?
A) Greece **B)** Turkey **C)** Egypt

4. What is the name of the Indonesian volcano that erupted with cataclysmic force in 1883?

5. Which two cities mark the start and end of the Trans-Siberian Railway?

6. The rice and beans dish *gallo pinto* (meaning 'red rooster') is the national dish of which Central American country?
A) Panama **B)** Belize **C)** Costa Rica

7. What two provinces were annexed from France by Germany in 1871 after the Franco-Prussian War, but then returned to France after the First World War?

8. Every year, tourists flock to Argentina's coast to watch an influx of which type of animal, which spends the winter there?
A) Whales **B)** Dolphins **C)** Butterflies

9. The Po is the longest river in which country?

10. Founded in around 400 BCE, Axum, one of the oldest continuously occupied cities in Africa, lies in which country?
A) Morocco **B)** Ethiopia **C)** Kenya

11. The Timor Sea lies off the north coast of which country?

12. Which mountain-living mammal of Central and South Asia is also known as an ounce?

13. What small Portuguese-speaking island nation lies off the west coast of Africa, around 250 km (155 miles) from Gabon?
A) São Tomé and Príncipe **B)** Madagascar
C) Réunion

14. The island of Malta is entirely lacking what natural features?
A) Beaches
B) Cliffs
C) Rivers

15. The Great Smoky Mountains National Park straddles Tennessee and which other US state?
A) North Carolina **B)** Kentucky **C)** Arkansas

16. Sometimes referred to as the 'Pearl of Asia', what is the capital city of Cambodia?

17. What famous annual sporting event is staged at Australia's Flemington Racecourse?

18. What country produces the greatest amount of milk?
A) China **B)** USA **C)** India

19. The overthrow of King James II of England and Scotland in 1688–89, and his replacement with William III and Mary II is often known by which two-word phrase?
A) Glorious Revolution **B)** Peasant's Revolt
C) Black Death

20. Which countries are these the internet domain names for? You get a point for each.
A) .br **B)** .ca **C)** .ch **D)** .cn **E)** .de **F)** .es
G) .ke **H)** .kr **I)** .ma **J)** .nz

Quiz 42 Film Locations

1. In which Italian city was Vittorio De Sica's *Bicycle Thieves* (1948) set and filmed?

2. In which US state would you find the Timberline Lodge, which provided the exterior shots for the hotel in Stanley Kubrick's *The Shining* (1980)?
A) Alaska B) Oregon C) Florida

3. Can you name the Austrian city where much of *The Sound of Music* (1965) was filmed?

4. Used as the temple of the Holy Grail in *Indiana Jones and the Last Crusade* (1989), the Treasury is a building in which historic Middle Eastern city?
A) Jerusalem B) Baghdad C) Petra

5. The 2008 film *Mamma Mia* was set on the fictional Greek island of Kalokairi. What real Greek island was used for filming?

6. But in the 2018 sequel, *Mamma Mia! Here We Go Again*, Kalokairi was recast as Vis, an island off the coast of which European country?

7. San Francisco is the setting for which 1958 film by Alfred Hitchcock?

8. Scotland's Glenfinnan viaduct features in four films from which major franchise?

9. The Thai island of Koh Phi Phi Leh provided the setting for which 2000 film starring Leonardo DiCaprio?

10. Most of the action in the 1959 Marilyn Monroe comedy *Some Like It Hot* takes place in Miami, Florida. But in which US city does the film begin?

11. The 1993 film *Jurassic Park* was set on the fictional Isla Nublar off the coast of which real Central American country?

12. And what real island chain was used for most of *Jurassic Park*'s location shots?

13. In what city is *Slumdog Millionaire* (2008) set?

14. The climatic scenes in the James Bond film *Skyfall* (2012) take place in 007's family home. In what country were these scenes filmed?

15. The hero of the Disney/Pixar film *Up* (2009) dreams of travelling to a fictional waterfall called 'Paradise Falls'. What real-life waterfall is it based on?

16. Wexford beach stood in for Normandy's Omaha beach during the filming of *Saving Private Ryan* (1998). In which country would you find Wexford beach?

17. Much of the *Godfather Part II* was filmed in which region of Italy, where the Corleone family was supposed to have come from?

18. Can you name the 1989 film that put Katz's Delicatessen in New York on the map?

19. The bleak landscape of Jordan's Wadi Rum provided the extraterrestrial backdrop for which 2015 film starring Matt Damon?

20. And let's finish with a three-part *Star Wars* location tester:
A) In what European country would you find the Hardangerjøkulen glacier which doubled as the ice planet Hoth in *The Empire Strikes Back*?
B) The Plaza de España, Seville, featured in which Star Wars film?
C) Luke Skywalker's fictional island hideaway in *The Force Awakens* and *The Last Jedi* was filmed on the real island of Skellig Michael off the coast of which European country?

Quiz 43 **General Knowledge**

1. The Shambles is a narrow medieval street in which English city?
A) York B) Liverpool C) Manchester

2. What is a vicuña?
A) A type of cactus B) A small four-footed mammal C) A maize-based alcoholic drink

3. 78.09% of Earth's atmosphere is made up of what gas?

4. The forint is the currency of which European country?
A) Hungary B) Romania C) Germany

5. The scientist Marie Curie, still the only person to win two Nobel prizes in separate sciences, was born in which country?

6. The Willis Tower (formerly the Sears Tower), the world's tallest building from 1973 to 1998, is in which US city?

7. What explorer gave the Pacific Ocean its name in 1520?

8. Who was the longest reigning pharaoh of ancient Egypt?
A) Ramses II B) Tutankhamun
C) Cleopatra VII

9. How many people have been to Space
A) Around 500 B) Around 5000
C) Around 50,000

10. The Large Hadron Collider, the world's most powerful particle accelerator, straddles the border between which two countries?

11. In what year did Tower Bridge in London open?
A) 1794 B) 1894 C) 1994

12. What is the largest state in India?
A) Rajasthan B) Uttar Pradesh C) Gujurat

13. In her novel *Cat's Eye*, Margaret Atwood describes which Canadian city as being like 'New York without the garbage and muggings'.
A) Montreal B) Toronto C) Vancouver

14. When people in the Congo basin talk of *mokole-mbembe*, what are they referring to?
A) A traditional Congolese dance
B) A species of baobab tree C) A dinosaur said to lurk in the Congolese forests

15. In 2000, Ecuador changed its currency from the sucre to what?
A) Peso B) Euro C) US dollar

16. The Indian Pacific is a passenger train service that runs for 4352 km (2704 miles) across which country?
A) India B) China C) Australia

17. New York's Solomon R. Guggenheim Museum (usually just known as The Guggenheim) was designed by which renowned 20th-century US architect?

18. What is this Australian geological formation called?
A) Hanging Rock B) Wave Rock
C) Ayers Rock

19. The Serengeti National Park is in which African country?
A) Kenya B) Tanzania C) Morocco

20. Name the five boroughs of New York City. You get a point for each.

© tbate54 / Shutterstock

Quiz 44 **General Knowledge**

1. If you're wandering around Dhaka spending some taka, where would you be?
A) India B) Pakistan C) Bangladesh

2. Making up the majority of plant species across the world, what distinguishes angiosperms from all other types of plants?
A) Bark B) Leaves C) Flowers

3. In what German city can you visit the house where the composer Ludwig van Beethoven was born?
A) Berlin B) Bonn C) Bremen

4. In what country is the tropical jungle known as the Daintree rainforest located?
A) Brazil B) Malaysia C) Australia

5. Flowing through Colombia and Venezuela, what is the fourth-largest river in the world, in terms of volume of water carried?
A) Orinoco B) River Plate C) Paraná

6. What is the only island where you can see lemurs in the wild?
A) Sri Lanka B) Iceland C) Madagascar

7. What is the national flower of the USA?
A) Sunflower B) Magnolia C) Rose

8. What is the third-largest country in Asia, by area, after Russia and China?

9. In Charles Dickens' novel *A Tale of Two Cities*, what are the two cities?

10. What is the capital and largest city of the US state of Hawaii?

11. Who or what was Quetzalcóatl to the Aztecs of Mexico?
A) Their capital city
B) A god who took the form of a feathered serpent
C) A currency based on cocoa beans

12. The Stoosbahn, the world's steepest funicular railway, is in which country?
A) Austria
B) Netherlands
C) Switzerland

13. What is the name of the world's largest tropical wetland, covering an area of around 195,000 sq km (75,000 sq miles), spread across parts of Brazil, Bolivia and Paraguay?

14. Tugela Falls is the highest waterfall on what continent? And, for a bonus point, what country is it in?

15. In what nation could you go for a stroll along the world's longest pleasure pier?
A) USA B) UK C) UAE

16. What is aloo, the key ingredient found in Indian dishes such as saag aloo, aloo gobi and aloo gosht?
A) Spinach
B) Potato
C) Cauliflower

17. 'Nollywood' is a term coined in the early 2000s to describe films produced in what country?
A) Norway B) Nigeria C) New Zealand

18. Goldeneye, Ian Fleming's holiday villa where he wrote most of the James Bond novels, is on which Caribbean island?
A) Jamaica B) Cuba C) Antigua

19. Which long-abandoned Middle Eastern city was described in 1845 by the English poet and clergyman John Burgon as 'a rose-red city half as old as time'?

20. Name the four presidents whose likenesses have been carved into Mt Rushmore. You get a point for each.

Answers on p.100   Score

Quiz 45 **General Knowledge**

1. The Spanish town of Buñol hosts an annual festival where people throw tonnes of what at each other?

2. In what city would you find Q1, which at 322.5 m (1058 ft) is the tallest building in Australia (and the second tallest structure in the southern hemisphere)?

3. The world's smallest bird, the bee hummingbird, lives only on which Caribbean island nation?
A) Cuba B) St Lucia C) Haiti

4. At the other end of the bird scale, what was the name of the giant flightless birds that once roamed New Zealand, but were hunted to extinction in the 15th century?

5. The cosmonaut Alexei Leonov was the first person to do what?
A) Orbit the Moon B) Walk in space
C) Live in a space station

6. What is the main ingredient of the Scandinavian dish *gravadlax* (or *gravlax*)?

7. The African Union has its headquarters in which city?
A) Cape Town, South Africa
B) Addis Ababa, Ethiopia C) Nairobi, Kenya

8. In what year did the *Titanic* sink?

9. The Italian Guglielmo Marconi is famous for inventing what?
A) The espresso machine
B) The battery C) Radio communication

10. The Serpentine is a lake in which London park?

11. Between 1932 and 1990, the Russian city of Nizhny Novgorod was named after which Soviet writer?

12. If you asked for an arepa in Venezuela, what would you be given?
A) A single bus ticket
B) A maize pancake C) A hat

13. What is the national flower of India?
A) Primrose B) Jasmine C) Lotus

14. Who became the first explorer to reach the South Pole in 1911?
A) Robert Falcon Scott B) Robert Peary
C) Roald Amundsen

15. The coffee chain Starbucks was founded in which US city?
A) Seattle B) New York C) San Francisco

16. What country is this?
A) Algeria B) Morocco C) Kenya

17. During the 1950s and 60s, Maria Bueno was one of Brazil's most successful sportspeople, in what field?
A) Motor racing B) Tennis C) Football

18. What constellation features on the flags of both Australia and New Zealand?

19. When was the first Tour de France held?
A) 1903 B) 1953 C) 1993

20. According to the US Census Bureau, what are the top 10 largest cities in the USA, by population? You get a point for each.

Answers on p.100   Score

Quiz 46 **Museums**

This one is simple: all you have to do is pick the city where the museum is located from the three options given.

1. World Museum, UK
A) Liverpool, England
B) Belfast, Northern Ireland
C) Edinburgh, Scotland

2. American Museum of Natural History
A) Los Angeles B) New York C) Chicago

3. Musée d'Orsay
A) Brussels, Belgium
B) Montreal, Canada
C) Paris, France

4. Victoria and Albert Museum, England
A) London B) Birmingham C) Manchester

5. Museo Nacional de Antropología
(National Museum of Anthropology)
A) Brasília, Brazil B) Mexico City, Mexico
C) Havana, Cuba

6. National Air and Space Museum of the
Smithsonian Institution, USA
A) New York B) San Francisco
C) Washington DC

7. National Museum of Australia
A) Sydney B) Melbourne C) Canberra

8. Apartheid Museum, South Africa
A) Johannesburg B) Cape Town C) Pretoria

9. Mouseio Akropolis (Acropolis Museum)
A) Athens, Greece
B) Cairo, Egypt
C) Istanbul, Turkey

10. Ghibli Museum
A) Beijing, China
B) Seoul, South Korea
C) Tokyo, Japan

11. National Museum of Nature and Science
A) Manila, Philippines
B) Seoul, South Korea
C) Tokyo, Japan

12. Museo Nacional Centro de Arte
Reina Sofía (Queen Sofía Museum), Spain
A) Barcelona B) Madrid C) Seville

13. National Museum of Brazil
A) Rio de Janeiro B) São Paulo C) Brasília

14. Capitoline Museums, Italy
A) Turin B) Siena C) Rome

15. House of Slaves
A) Monrovia, Liberia,
B) Dakar, Senegal
C) Freetown, Sierra Leone

16. Museum of New Zealand Te
Papa Tongarewa
A) Auckland B) Wellington C) Christchurch

17. El Museo del Oro (Museum of Gold)
A) Bogotá, Colombia
B) Caracas, Venezuela
C) Panama City, Panama

18. National Museum of China
A) Hong Kong B) Shanghai C) Beijing

19. Blue Penny Museum
A) Port Louis, Mauritius
B) Antananarivo, Madagascar
C) Saint-Denis, Réunion

20. Chilean National Museum of Fine Arts
A) Valparaíso
B) Santiago
C) Puente Alto

Quiz 47 **General Knowledge**

1. What is the longest river in Asia?

2. The Massachusetts island of Martha's Vineyard stood in for the fictional resort of Amity Island in which classic 1970s film?

3. Boulders Beach, home to a colony of African penguins that have become a major tourist draw, is on the outskirts of which South African city?

4. What is the tallest building in the world?
A) Shanghai Tower, China
B) The Shard, London, UK
C) Burj Khalifa, Dubai, UAE

5. What country has won more Winter Olympic medals than any other?
A) Germany B) Norway C) USA

6. In what country is the source of the Amazon River?

7. One of Scotland's most popular tourist attractions, the Kelvingrove Art Gallery can be found in what city?

8. What did the underwater archaeologist Robert Ballard discover in 1985 around 600 km (370 miles) from the coast of Newfoundland, Canada?

9. Some of the world's earliest civilisations were established in the Middle Eastern area of Mesopotamia, which lies between which two rivers?

10. What record does the US astronaut Eugene Cernan hold?
A) He has spent the most number of days in space
B) He has flown further from Earth than any other astronaut
C) He was the last person on the Moon

11. People in Mexico often celebrate the annual Day of the Dead Festival by giving *calaveras* as gifts or offerings. What is a *calavera*?

12. If you're catching a flight from LHR to LAX, which two cities (and airports) will you be travelling between?

13. In 1980, the New Hebrides island group in the South Pacific changed its name to what?
A) New Scotland B) Fiji C) Vanuatu

14. Geologists believe that around 335 million years ago all the continents were joined together into one giant supercontinent known as what?

15. Built on an artificial offshore island, Kansai International Airport serves which Japanese city?
A) Tokyo B) Osaka C) Sapporo

16. Growing to over a metre (3 ft) in length and found in the wetlands of South America, what is the world's largest rodent?

17. Roughly what percentage of Austria is mountainous?
A) 30% B) 45% C) 60%

18. The world's second-longest barrier reef lies mainly off the coast of Mexico and which Central American country?
A) Belize B) El Salvador C) Panama

19. Who was Emperor of Ethiopia from 1930 to 1974, and is regarded as a god by followers of the Rastafari religion?

20. Can you name Europe's eight Alpine nations, whose territory encompasses part of the continent's highest mountain range? You get a point for each.

Quiz 48 **General Knowledge**

1. The rickshaw is believed to have been invented in the 1860s in which country?
A) Japan B) Thailand C) The Philippines

2. What is the only continent where the large flightless birds known as rheas can be seen in the wild?

3. The archipelago of Madeira, lying off the north-west coast of Africa, belongs to which country?

4. If you wanted to run up the Rocky Steps, just like Sylvester Stallone did in the 1976 movie, what US city should you visit?

5. Last visible from Earth in 1986, when will Halley's comet next pay us a visit?
A) 2061 B) 2161 C) 2261

6. What is the capital of South Australia?

7. Sharm El Sheikh is an Egyptian city and resort on which body of water?

8. What is Europe's largest and busiest port?
A) Rotterdam, Netherlands
B) Hamburg, Germany C) Valencia, Spain

9. Antietam, Bull Run and Shiloh were battles in which war?
A) US Civil War B) Boer War C) First World War

10. Prince Siddhartha, the founder of Buddhism, was born in which country?
A) China B) India C) Japan

11. *Pan troglodytes* is the scientific name of which African great ape?
A) Common chimpanzee B) Lowland gorilla
C) Hamadryas baboon

12. Completed in 1970, the Aswan Dam was built across which river?
A) Nile B) Danube C) Amazon

13. Which planet has the longest day?

14. Georges Bizet's opera *Carmen* centres on the bawdy adventures of a tobacco factory worker in which Spanish city?

15. Today found only in India and Nepal, what sort of animal is a gharial?
A) A monkey B) A bird C) A reptile

16. The Moche and the Wari are ancient civilizations that once flourished on which continent?

17. What is the name of this palace complex?

18. The Italian liqueur amaretto is traditionally flavoured with what?

19. In 1993, as an alternative to the Easter bunny, Australian shops started offering chocolate likenesses of what animal in order to raise awareness of the plight of native wildlife?
A) Kangaroo B) Koala C) Bilby

20. Match the airport to the airport code:
Airports: A) Berlin Tegel B) Chicago O'Hare
C) London Stansted D) Montréal–Pierre Elliott Trudeau E) Newark Liberty
F) Rio de Janeiro–Antônio Carlos Jobim
G) Washington Dulles

Codes: IAD, GIG, EWR, YUL, STN, ORD, TXL

Quiz 49 **The World of Books**

Test your literary knowledge with this global book tour.

1. The *Great Railway Bazaar* (1975) is an account of an epic four-month train journey from London to Southeast Asia, and back again, by which renowned travel writer?
A) Bruce Chatwin
B) Bill Bryson
C) Paul Theroux

2. Christopher Isherwood's 1930s novel *Goodbye to Berlin* was turned into what musical (later a film starring Liza Minnelli) by the composers Kander and Ebb in the 1960s?

3. John Kennedy Toole's *A Confederacy of Dunces* (1980) concerns the adventures of Ignatius J. Reilly in which US City?
A) New Orleans
B) Miami
C) Charleston

4. Ben Okri, author of the award-winning novel *The Famished Road* (1991) is from which African country?
A) South Africa
B) Egypt
C) Nigeria

5. *High Adventure* (1955) was whose account of a famous climb?

6. Irvine Welsh's novel *Trainspotting* (1993) is set in which British city?
A) London
B) Cardiff
C) Edinburgh

7. *One Hundred Years of Solitude* (1967) and *Love in the Time of Cholera* (1985) are among the works of which celebrated Colombian novelist?

8. What is the name of Harper Lee's debut novel, set in Alabama?

9. *Ten Days That Shook the World* (1919) is the American journalist John Reed's account of which momentous 20th-century event?
A) Death of Queen Victoria
B) Outbreak of the First World War
C) The Russian Revolution

10. What was the award-winning 1997 debut novel of the Indian writer, Arundhati Roy?
A) *A Suitable Boy*
B) *The God of Small Things*
C) *The Ministry of Utmost Happiness*

11. The inhabitants of which city's slums did the British writer George Orwell describe as 'a gathering-place for eccentric people – people who have fallen into solitary, half-mad grooves of life and given up trying to be normal or decent.'
A) Paris
B) London
C) Wigan

12. What 2004 novel by Haruki Murakami takes place in Tokyo over the course of a single night?
A) *Norwegian Wood*
B) *After Dark*
C) *The Wind-Up Bird Chronicle*

13. What famous travel writer was born in Des Moines, Iowa?
A) P.J. O'Rourke
B) Bill Bryson
C) Eric Newby

14. The events of the novel *Treasure Island* (1882) by Robert Louis Stevenson begin at the Admiral Benbow Inn on the outskirts of which British city?
A) Liverpool
B) Bristol
C) Glasgow

15. What city was Fyodor Dostoevsky describing in his 1866 novel *Crime and Punishment* when he wrote: 'This is a city of half-crazy people... there are few places where you'll find so many gloomy, harsh and strange influences on the soul of a man.'
A) Berlin
B) Moscow
C) St Petersburg

16. Ernest Hemingway's *The Old Man and the Sea* (1952) tells the story of a struggle with a giant marlin by a fisherman from which country?
A) USA
B) Cuba
C) Mexico

17. What links *Le Morte d'Arthur* (1485) by Thomas Malory, *Don Quixote* (1615) by Miguel de Cervantes, *The Pilgrim's Progress* (1678) by John Bunyon, and *De Profundis* (1905) by Oscar Wilde?
A) They have almost identical plots
B) The were published on the same day of the year
C) They were all written in prison (at least in part)

18. Marlon James, whose novel *A Brief History of Seven Killings* won the 2015 Man Booker Prize, is from which country?
A) Jamaica
B) USA
C) UK

19. Which American writer said of Jane Austen, 'Every time I read *Pride and Prejudice* I want to dig her up and beat her over the skull with her own shin-bone'?
A) Ogden Nash
B) Mark Twain
C) Henry James

20. From what country did Agatha Christie's finickity detective Hercule Poirot come from?
A) Belgium
B) France
C) India

21. In 1776, the first instalment of what six-volume masterwork by the English writer Edward Gibbon was published?
A) *The Oxford English Dictionary*
B) *The Encyclopaedia Britannica*
C) *The History of the Decline and Fall of the Roman Empire*

22. The Millennium trilogy of thrillers, which begins with *The Girl with the Dragon Tattoo*, was written by which Swedish author?

23. The narrator of Salman Rushdie's multi-award-winning novel *Midnight's Children* was born at exactly the same time as what major event?
A) The Second World War ended
B) The first atomic bomb exploded
C) India became an independent country

24. What is the name of the 2007 novel by Junot Díaz set in the Dominican Republic that won the 2008 Pulitzer Prize for Fiction?
A) *The Road*
B) *The Brief Wondrous Life of Oscar Wao*
C) *Portnoy's Complaint*

25. The author of the comic novel, *My Uncle Napoleon* (1973), Iraj Pezeshkzad hails from which country?
A) Iraq
B) Iran
C) France

Quiz 50 **General Knowledge**

1. In what year was the first Venice Film Festival held?
A) 1932 B) 1962 C) 2002

2. Haneda Airport serves which major Asian city?

3. Who was the charismatic (and controversial) Marxist president of Venezuela from 2002 until his death in 2013?

4. The popular tourist and cruise-liner destination of Montego Bay is on the north coast of which Caribbean island?

5. Roughly how many people live in the island country of Fiji in the Pacific Ocean?
A) 90,000 B) 900,000 C) 9 million

6. The wireless technology Bluetooth is named after what or who?
A) A record-breaking 19th-century sailing ship that could travel between countries in super-fast time
B) The Danish King Harald Gormsson, famed for bringing his country's warring tribes together into a single kingdom
C) A type of creeping plant that rapidly spreads between forest trees

7. By what name is the small statue of a urinating boy – one of Brussels' top tourist attractions – officially known?

8. In what year was the first transatlantic telegraph cable completed?
A) 1858 B) 1898 C) 1958

9. The Henry Wood Promenade Concerts, held each summer at London's Royal Albert Hall, are better known by what name?

10. In what country could you visit Tongariro National Park?
A) UK B) Zambia C) New Zealand

11. Iceland produces most of its energy through what?
A) Geothermal energy B) Hydropower
C) Burning whale blubber

12. The tusk of which marine mammal can grow up to 3.1 m (10.2 ft)?

13. Lying over 3800 m (12,500 ft) above sea level in the Andes, what lake (the highest to be navigable) borders Bolivia and Peru?

14. In what part of the world did bananas originate?
A) South America B) Southeast Asia
C) Europe

15. Nicolae Ceauşescu was overthrown as the leader of what country in 1989?

16. What is the name of the Florida space centre from which almost every manned US space flight has been launched?
A) Kennedy B) Reagan C) Bush

17. Which iconic Italian structure was completed in 1372, 199 years after it was begun?
A) The Colosseum B) Florence Cathedral
C) The Leaning Tower of Pisa

18. In the late 19th century, the former slave Toussaint Louverture led the revolution that ended with the establishment of which Caribbean country?
A) Haiti B) Jamaica C) Cuba

19. What is an orrery?
A) A mechanical model of the solar system
B) A traditional Portuguese dish
C) A type of French boat

20. The Nile flows through 11 African countries. How many can you name? You get a point for each.

Answers on p.102 Score

Quiz 51 General Knowledge

1. What special venue is used for the annual summer opera festival in the town of Orange in southern France?
A) A giant vat of oranges
B) A Roman amphitheatre
C) A floating temporary stage on a lake

2. Josip Broz Tito was the former leader of which former country?

3. What popular team sport was invented by the Canadian physical education teacher Dr James Naismith in 1891 as a way of keeping his pupils occupied on a rainy day?

4. The Don Juan Pond, the most salty body of water in the world, is located on which continent?
A) Antarctica B) Asia C) Australia

5. The Indian company Bajaj Auto is the world's largest manufacturer of what form of transport?
A) Autorickshaws B) Coracles C) Gliders

6. Roughly how many Caribbean islands are there?
A) Around 700 B) Around 7000
C) Around 17,000

7. What 19th-century statesman, who oversaw the unification of Germany in 1871, was known as the 'Iron Chancellor'?

8. Name the country from these clues: it was established in 1923 from the remnants of a recently collapsed empire; it straddles two continents; most of the population are Muslims; it's a member of NATO; its largest city is not its capital.

9. The US dam that borders Nevada and Arizona and created Lake Mead, the country's largest reservoir, is named after what former president?

10. In 1961, India annexed the coastal state of Goa from which European power, which had effectively ruled it for over four centuries?

11. By what name was the modern Egyptian city of Luxor known in ancient times?
A) Memphis B) Thebes C) Alexandria

12. The 2002 film *City of God* focused on the growth of organised crime between the 1960s and the 1980s in which city?

13. What's the tallest mountain on the mainland of Australia?

14. The Scottish seaman Alexander Selkirk, who spent four years from 1704 to 1709 marooned on a South Pacific island, was supposedly the inspiration behind what book, published in 1719?

15. What is the name of the flatbread traditionally served with Ethiopian meals?
A) Wat B) Injera C) Niter kibbeh

16. The Romans sited their capital in Britain at Camulodunum, which is still a thriving city, although what name does it go by today?

17. What part of Oceania takes its name from the Greek for 'many islands'?

18. How many moons does the planet Mercury have?

19. The *New Colossus* is a poem inscribed upon what well-known US landmark?

20. Name the countries for which these cities are the capital? You get a point for each:
A) Bridgetown B) Tegucigalpa C) Quito
D) Asunción E) Ljubljana F) Tirana
G) Luanda H) Dar es Salaam
I) Colombo J) Port Moresby

Answers on p.102   Score

Quiz 52 **General Knowledge**

1. Named after a Cuban beach, a daiquiri cocktail contains lime juice, sugar syrup and what other crucial alcoholic ingredient?

2. India's Golden Triangle is tourist circuit made up of three of the country's most visited cities: Delhi (the capital), Agra (site of the Taj Mahal) and which other city?

3. What pattern features on the jersey of the cyclist awarded the title of 'King of the Mountains' in the Tour de France?

4. Which is the only continent where you can see jackass penguins living in the wild?

5. In 1853, Commander Matthew Perry arrived with several large warships off the coast of which country, which he intended to force into a trading relationship with the USA?

6. What is the main difference between the Italian soft cheeses, marscapone and ricotta?

7. Prior to human settlement, what was the only type of mammal inhabiting New Zealand's mainland?

8. Located in Bolivia, what is the Salar de Uyuni?
A) The ruins of an ancient settlement
B) The world's largest salt flat
C) A modernist sculpture park

9. Boonoo Boonoo, Capoompeta, Paroo-Darling, and the Warrumbungle are national parks in which country?

10. What Spanish city has a name that means 'pomegranate'?

11. What was the name of the ship on which Charles Darwin travelled around the world conducting the research that would lead him to formulate his theories of evolution?

12. The longest yearly migration in the animal kingdom is performed by which animal?
A) Dingo B) Green turtle C) Arctic tern

13. Offa's Dyke runs along the border between which two European countries?

14. What iconic US building is this?

15. What famous song was written by Claude Joseph Rouget de Lisle in 1792 to mark France declaring war on Austria?

16. How many times has Argentina won the FIFA World Cup?

17. One of the busiest shipping lanes in the world, the Strait of Malacca lies between which two Asian countries?
A) China and the Philippines B) South Korea and Japan C) Malaysia and Indonesia

18. There are 287 languages spoken in Europe. Roughly, how many are spoken in Africa?
A) 215 B) 2150 C) 21,500

19. If your plane ticket says you're travelling from JFK to CDG, what two cities would you be flying between?

20. Including the prototype, NASA built six space shuttles which operated between 1976 (the first test flight) and 2011 (the final orbital flight). How many can you name? You get a point for each.

© meunierd / Shutterstock

Quiz 53 Space

1. What gas gives the planets Uranus and Neptune their blue colour?
A) Hydrogen B) Methane C) Helium

2. What does the acronym NASA stand for?

3. What is the name of the space transportation company founded by the entrepreneur Elon Musk in 2002?

4. What is the name of the space telescope launched in 1990, which has given us unprecedented views of the universe?

5. What sort of star is the Sun?
A) White dwarf B) Yellow dwarf C) Red giant

6. 'Dirty snowballs' (or 'snowy dirt balls') are nicknames given to which celestial objects?

7. What was the name of the US space station launched in 1973, which fell back to Earth in 1979?
A) Kosmos B) Mir C) Skylab

8. Roughly how long ago did the solar system form?
A) 6000 years ago
B) 4.6 billion years ago
C) 13.7 billion years ago

9. Who or what is the planet Mars named after?

10. Elliptical, spiral and lenticular are all types of what celestial feature?

11. Roscosmos is the space agency of which country?
A) Japan B) Russia C) India

12. What was the first planet to be visited by a spacecraft from Earth? And, for a bonus point, in what year?

13. The lumps and particles that make up Saturn's rings are mainly composed of what material?
A) Rock
B) Water ice
C) Frozen hydrogen

14. Roughly speaking, what speed does a rocket have to be travelling at in order to break free of Earth's gravity and go into space?
A) 20,000 kph (12,500 mph)
B) 30,000 kph (19,000 mph)
C) 40,000 kph (25,000 mph)

15. What is the average temperature of the Sun's core?
A) 5600°C (10,100°F)
B) 1.5 million°C (2.7 million°F)
C) 15 million°C (27 million°F)

16. What's the scientific name for the northern and southern lights – the shimmering patterns in the sky, caused by solar particles reacting with the atmosphere?

17. What is the rain on Venus made of?
A) Water B) Sulphuric acid
C) Frozen methane

18. What fairy-tale-inspired term do scientists use to describe an area of space that has just the right conditions to support life?

19. What is an exoplanet?
A) An extremely large planet
B) A planet destroyed in a supernova
C) A planet orbiting a star in a solar system other than our own

20. In which direction does Earth spin?
A) From east to west
B) From west to east
C) From top to bottom

Answers on p.103   Score

Quiz 54 **General Knowledge**

1. Every year, a mass migration of red crabs blocks the roads of which Pacific island?
A) Christmas Island **B)** Easter island
C) Thanksgiving Island

2. Turkey's Bosphorus Strait connects the Sea of Marmara and the Mediterranean Sea with which inland body of water?

3. The Calcutta Cup is an (almost) annual rugby match between which two countries?

4. The 250 sq km (97 sq mile) Perito Moreno Glacier is a popular tourist attraction in which South American country?

5. What island nation is Asia's smallest country, by both area and population?
A) The Maldives **B)** Sri Lanka **C)** Japan

6. What is the name of the ancient Greek mathematician (c. 287–212 BCE) best known for leaping from his bath and running through the streets naked, shouting 'Eureka' ('I have it!').

7. Found in the icy waters of the Arctic Ocean, the vertebrate species with the longest known lifespan is a type of what?
A) Turtle **B)** Shark **C)** Whale

8. What country has the highest number of Unesco World Heritage Sites?
A) Italy **B)** China **C)** Mexico

9. Raymond Chandler's Philip Marlowe novels were (mostly) set in which US city?

10. Indonesia's Spice Islands, the original source of nutmeg, mace and cloves (which once grew only there), are more properly known by what name?

11. What famous annual US horse race lasts just two minutes (approximately)?

12. What European capital city is home to the Musical Instruments Museum (or MIM for short)?

13. In which country would you find the Orapa mine, the world's largest diamond mine?
A) Russia **B)** Botswana **C)** Australia

14. What is the name of Mexico's earliest civilisation, best known for its carvings of giant stone heads?
A) Olmecs **B)** Zapotecs **C)** Toltecs

15. The only surviving member of an ancient line of reptiles that goes back more than 200 million years to the time of the dinosaurs, the lizard-like tuatara is native to which country?

16. What is the area in France formed by the delta of the River Rhône, which is famed for its animals, particularly a breed of white horses?

17. What is the hottest planet in the solar system?
A) Mercury **B)** Venus **C)** Neptune

18. What was the capital city of the Inca Empire?
A) Lima **B)** Cuzco **C)** Machu Picchu

19. What is the name of the enormous trench in East Africa, several thousand kilometres long, marking the boundary where tectonic movement is gradually splitting Africa apart?

20. Which cities do the following international airports serve?
You get a point for each.
A) O'Hare **B)** Dulles **C)** Ministro Pistarini
D) Jorge Chávez **E)** George Best **F)** John Lennon **G)** Leonardo da Vinci **H)** Jomo Kenyatta **I)** Narita **J)** Kingsford Smith

Quiz 55 **General Knowledge**

1. The furthest humans have ever travelled from Earth is 400,171 km (248,655 miles) during which of the Apollo missions?
A) Apollo 11 **B)** Apollo 13 **C)** Apollo 17

2. The Italian city of Siena has been famed since medieval times for its *palio*. What is the Palio di Siena?
A) An archery competition **B)** A horse race
C) A wine festival

3. Montevideo is the capital of what country?

4. What is the only one of the original seven ancient wonders for which no archaeological evidence has been found?

5. 'Catatumbo Lightning' is a phenomenon in which the mouth of the Catatumbo River enjoys intense lightning storms lasting up to nine hours around 260 days a year. Where is mouth of the Catatumbo River?

6. Which of the seven continents has the fastest growing population?

7. The Uros people of Peru live where?
A) In abandoned Inca sites
B) Nowhere permanently; they are a nomadic people
C) On floating islands made of reeds on Lake Titicaca

8. In what country would you find the city of Batman?
A) Australia **B)** USA **C)** Turkey

9. What is the world's most common bird?

10. If you ordered a *medianoche* in a Cuban restaurant, what would you be served?

11. If your airplane luggage tag has you down as flying from LGW to CPT, from where and to where are you travelling?

12. The world's longest land border lies between which two countries?
A) Argentina and Chile
B) Russia and Kazakhstan
C) USA and Canada

13. Common in Antarctica, where there are an estimated 15 million individuals, the crabeater seal mainly feeds on what?
A) Crabs **B)** Lobster **C)** Krill

14. Which Scottish city is known as the 'Granite City'?

15. According to figures gathered by the NCIS (National Coronial Information System), what animals were responsible for the greatest number of deaths in Australia between 2000 and 2010?
A) Snakes **B)** Sharks **C)** Kangaroos
D) Dogs **E)** Horses

16. Hooded, American hog-nosed, and striped are all species of what type of mammal, found in the Americas?

17. Waterloo, the site of Napoleon Bonaparte's last battle in 1815, is in which European country?

18. Which country would you be looking at through your carriage windows if you were riding on the BAM railway?
A) Belgium **B)** Chile **C)** Russia

19. The peach melba dessert was invented by the French chef Auguste Escoffier to honour an opera singer from which country?

20. In which countries were the following airlines founded? You get a point for each.
A) Qantas **B)** Gulf Air **C)** Etihad
D) Lufthansa **E)** El Al **F)** Aer Lingus
G) Air Astana **H)** KLM
I) Tarom **J)** Conviasa

Answers on p.104   Score

Quiz 56 **Landmarks**

1. In one of history's great scams, what famous landmark did André Poisson buy for scrap from Victor Lustig in 1922?
A) The Eiffel Tower
B) The Statue of Liberty
C) Sydney Harbour Bridge

2. In what many people believe to have been a scam (but wasn't), what famous landmark was dismantled and re-erected in Lake Havasu City, Arizona, in 1971?
A) The Great Pyramid
B) London Bridge
C) Stonehenge

3. Once the largest sports stadium in the world, and still the biggest in Brazil, what is the football stadium in Rio de Janeiro that hosted both the 1950 and 2014 World Cup Finals, as well as the opening and closing ceremonies of the 2016 Summer Olympics?

4. What famous New York landmark was the subject of an eight-hour film by Andy Warhol in 1964?
A) The Flat Iron Building
B) The Chrysler Building
C) The Empire State Building

5. What and where is this building?

6. What is the name of the large church – once the world's largest – in the Vatican City?

7. The Great Barrier Reef lies off the coast of which Australian state?
A) New South Wales
B) Queensland
C) Western Australia

8. The bell tower that forms part of the British Houses of Parliament complex is often referred to as Big Ben. Technically, however, that named should be used only for what?
A) The clock face B) The bell C) The roof

9. The lowest point in North America, 86 m (282 ft) below sea level, and one of the hottest places in the world, Death Valley is located in which US state?

10. Situated in Russia, The Motherland Calls, one of the world's largest statues, commemorates which battle? And, for a bonus point, in what city is it?

11. What world-famous landmark, built between 1632 and 1653, required over 1000 elephants to deliver its building materials?
A) Hampton Court
B) The Parthenon
C) The Taj Mahal

12. Can you name the Las Vegas hotel, shaped like an Egyptian pyramid, from whose summit shines the world's most powerful light?
A) MGM Grand
B) The Bellagio
C) The Luxor

13. What is the name of the church, topped with colourful onion domes, on the south side of Moscow's Red Square?
A) St Basil's Cathedral
B) St Augustine's Cathedral
C) St Paul's Cathedral

14. What mountain is this?

15. The Sky Tower, the tallest structure in the southern hemisphere, is located in which city?
A) Sydney, Australia
B) Buenos Aires, Argentina
C) Auckland, New Zealand

16. What is the name of the fairy-tale castle built by Ludwig II of Bavaria in the late 19th century?
A) Neuschwanstein Castle
B) Bled Castle
C) Windsor Castle

17. The mansion Graceland, once owned by Elvis Presley and now a major tourist attraction, is in which US state?
A) Mississippi
B) Tennessee
C) California

18. What is the region of the Colorado Plateau, dotted with large sandstone formations, which formed the backdrop to many westerns from the 1930s to 1950s – particularly those of director John Ford?

19. Begun in 532 by the Eastern Roman Emperor Justinian I, the Aya Sofya is a large, multi-domed building in which city?
A) Athens, Greece
B) Paris, France
C) Istanbul, Turkey

20. What Unesco World Heritage site is Peru's most visited tourist attraction?

21. How many years did it take to build New York's Brooklyn Bridge?
A) 1
B) 14
C) 27

22. What and where is this?

23. What is the name of the vast temple complex, the largest religious monument in the world, built in the 12th century in what is now Cambodia?

24. The Parthenon in Athens, Greece, is a fifth-century BCE temple dedicated to which deity?
A) Zeus
B) Athena
C) Shiva

25. Built by the pharaoh Ramses II in the 13th century BCE, what happened to the Abu Simbel temple complex in 1968?
A) It was destroyed in an earthquake
B) It was relocated to make way for the Aswan Dam reservoir
C) It was buried by a sandstorm

Answers on p.105   Score

Quiz 57 **General Knowledge**

1. What is the easternmost state in the USA?
A) Florida B) North Carolina C) Maine

2. In what Spanish city was the painter Pablo Picasso born? It's now home to a museum dedicated to his work.
A) Madrid B) Málaga C) Seville

3. The Shakespeare play *Romeo and Juliet* is set in which European city?

4. Though physically separated from it, Kaliningrad is part of what country?

5. In 1770, which explorer became the first European to reach the east coast of Australia, claiming the land for Britain?

6. What African capital city is this?

7. Once estimated to have a wild population of over five billion, what bird was hunted to extinction in North America in the 19th century?

8. In Japan, what is a netsuke?
A) A salad made with both raw and cooked fish
B) A slow, regional train that makes multiple stops
C) A small carved ornament used for attaching objects to the sash of a kimono

9. What's the windiest planet in the solar system, where gusts can reach in excess of 2000 kph (1200 mph)?

10. In 1637, there was a sudden surge in demand for what natural product in the Netherlands, which saw prices rocket to astronomical levels before crashing to next to nothing in just a few weeks?

11. Released in 1906, *The Story of the Kelly Gang* is generally recognised to be the first feature-length film ever made. In what country was it produced?

12. The vast, 1441-room baroque Schönbrunn Palace, a former imperial residence, is situated in which European capital city?

13. In what year was the online peer-to-peer property rental company Airbnb founded?
A) 1998 B) 2008 C) 2012

14. Found in the rivers and waterways of Australia, Southern Asia and Southeast Asia, what is the largest reptile in the world?

15. Accra is the capital and largest city of which African country?

16. Where was the world's first stock exchange established?
A) London B) Amsterdam C) New York

17. General Pinochet overthrew the democratically elected Salvador Allende to become dictator of which country in 1973?

18. What vegetable is the main ingredient of the Russian/East European soup, borscht?

19. Of the 19 US Smithsonian museums, 17 are located in which US city? And, for a bonus point, around which park are 11 of these museums situated?

20. How many of the eight countries that share a land border with Turkey can you name? You get a point for each.

Answers on p.105   Score

Quiz 58 **General Knowledge**

1. How many countries make up Africa?
A) 34 B) 54 C) 74

2. What is the only South American country where Dutch is the official language?

3. What is the name of the landlocked Southeast Asian country bordered by China, Vietnam, Cambodia, Thailand and Myanmar?

4. The Plimsoll Line on the side of a ship marks what?
A) The position of the ship's engines
B) The storeroom for the crew's shoes
C) The maximum depth the ship may be safely immersed in water

5. And what does the Karman Line mark?
A) The boundary between the waters of the Atlantic and Pacific oceans
B) The boundary between Earth's atmosphere and outer space
C) The boundary between the Earth's solid crust and the molten rock of the mantle

6. Vaduz is the capital of which small European country?

7. If you are taking a ride on the passenger train service known as the Ghan, what country are you crossing?

8. Until 1982, Harare, the capital of Zimbabwe, was known by what name?

9. The Vince Lombardi Trophy is awarded to the winner of what sporting competition?

10. What insect has the biggest wings, in terms of the overall surface area?
A) Hercules moth B) Titan beetle
C) Queen Alexandra Birdwing

11. Alto Douro is a wine region in which European country?

12. Featuring performances by Janis Joplin, Jimi Hendrix and The Who, the Woodstock festival of 1969 was staged on a dairy farm just north of which US city?

13. In what part of the world would you find the Sunda Islands?
A) Antarctica B) Australia C) Southeast Asia

14. What world-famous building is this?

15. Stratus clouds typically appear as what?
A) A low grey (or white) blanket
B) Thin, high-altitude wisps
C) Fluffy clouds at a medium altitude

16. The dinosaurs died out at the end of what geological period?
A) Triassic B) Jurassic C) Cretaceous

17. Doric, Ionic and Corinthian were the three main styles of what in ancient Greece?
A) Architecture B) Food C) Hairstyle

18. What is South America's largest flying bird?
A) Andean condor B) Giant toucan C) Rhea

19. Suva is the capital of which Pacific island nation?

20. Can you name the top 10 most visited countries in the world (according to 2016 figures)? You get a point for each.

Answers on p.106   Score

Quiz 59 **Transport**

1. Garuda is the national airline of which country?
A) Guyana
B) Indonesia
C) Gabon

2. The Blue Train is a luxurious train service that makes a 1600 km (990 mile) journey across which country? And, for a couple of bonus points, what two cities does it travel between?

3. According to World Bank figures, what country has the most number of cars per person in the world?
A) USA
B) Monaco
C) San Marino

4. The End of the World Train, considered the most southerly functioning railway in the world, operates at the tip of which country?
A) New Zealand
B) Argentina
C) South Africa

5. *Oasis of the Seas*, *Freedom of the Seas*, *Monarch of the Seas*, *Harmony of the Seas* and various other ships with 'of the seas' suffixes are all cruise liners owned and operated by which company?
A) P&O
B) Royal Caribbean International
C) Tesla

6. What transport record does a 1990s German-built vehicle called the Bagger 293 hold?
A) It has the world's most powerful diesel engine
B) It is the heaviest moving land vehicle ever made
C) It's the world's largest motorbike

7. The world's first underground railway opened in 1863 in which city?
A) London
B) Paris
C) Budapest

8. With the largest wingspan of any plane ever built (97.54 m/320 ft), the *Spruce Goose* was designed by which famous business magnate and film producer?

9. What speed did the jet-propelled car *ThrustSSC* set when it broke the land-speed record in 1997?
A) 888 kph (553 mph)
B) 1028 kph (639 mph)
C) 1228 kph (763 mph)

10. The first manned hot-air balloon flight took place in 1783, in what country?
A) France
B) Scotland
C) China

11. Japanese high-speed Shinkansen trains are also known by what nickname?

12. Over 21 billion km (13.2 billion miles) away and travelling at an astonishing 62,140 kph (38,500 mph), what spacecraft is the furthest human-made object from Earth?

13. What pioneering form of transport did Richard Trevithick invent?
A) The steam locomotive
B) The solar-powered plane
C) The four-wheel-drive car

14. The first military submarine was used in which conflict?
A) The American War of Independence
B) The Crimean War
C) The First World War

© Skycolors / Shutterstock

15. What European engineer is generally credited with the invention of the motor car?

16. What is the name of the British locomotive that in 1938 set a world speed record for a steam train of 203 kph (126 mph) that still stands today?
A) *Flying Scotsman*
B) *Mallard*
C) *Union Pacific*

17. What transport first took place on 17 December 1903 at Kitty Hawk, North Carolina, USA?

18. How long was the longest ever train?
A) 1.8 km (1.11 miles)
B) 4.1 km (2.54 miles)
C) 7.3 km (4.53 miles)

19. What sort of plane is this?
A) Airbus 320
B) Boeing 747 'Jumbo Jet'
C) Learjet 23

20. In 1737, the English clockmaker John Harrison developed one of the most influential transport devices of all time, a marine chronometer that finally allowed sailors to accurately calculate what?

21. According to the song, what service departs from Pennsylvania Station's Track 29?

22. What is the world's busiest airport?
A) Hartsfield-Jackson Atlanta International Airport
B) Beijing Capital International Airport, China
C) Dubai International Airport, United Arab Emirates

23. With the tallest of its towers reaching a height of 343 m (1125 ft), the Millau Viaduct is the world's tallest bridge. In what country would you find it?
A) USA
B) Italy
C) France

24. What is currently (as of 2018) the longest scheduled flight?
A) Qatar Airways: Auckland, New Zealand, to Doha, Qatar
B) Qantas Airways: Perth, Australia, to London, UK
C) Emirates Airways: Auckland, New Zealand, to Dubai, UAE

25. What countries have the following international vehicle registration codes? You get a point for each.
i) A
ii) AUS
iii) BR
iv) C
v) CDN
vi) CI
vii) E
viii) FJI
ix) GB
x) J
xi) NZ
xii) RA
xiii) ROK
xiv) USA
xv) ZA

Quiz 60 **General Knowledge**

1. In what country would you find the ancient city of Timbuktu?
A) Mali B) Chad C) Greece

2. What body of water separates Australia from New Zealand?
A) Sea of Japan
B) Tasman Sea
C) Indian Ocean

3. Which of these countries isn't located on the Equator?
A) Kenya B) Brazil C) India

4. What fast-food company, founded in 1965 in Connecticut, USA, now has more outlets worldwide (42,000) than any other?
A) McDonald's B) Nando's C) Subway

5. The flag of which country is coloured green, white and red, with a central emblem depicting an eagle on a cactus eating a snake?
A) Mexico B) Canada C) Barbados

6. What is the largest country in Africa, by area?
A) South Africa B) Nigeria C) Algeria

7. And what is the largest country in Africa, by population?
A) South Africa B) Nigeria C) Algeria

8. What is the most sparsely populated country in Europe, with an average of just 17 people per square kilometre?
A) Finland B) Norway C) Greece

9. Roughly, how many species of tree grow in the Amazon rainforest?
A) 600 B) 1600 C) 16,000

10. How many times could the UK fit whole into Russia?
A) 6 B) 69 C) 169

11. In what Italian region is the country's capital, Rome, located?
A) Abruzzo
B) Emilia-Romagna
C) Lazio

12. What is the largest hotel in the world in terms of the number of rooms?
A) First World Hotel, Malaysia
B) The Venetian, Las Vegas, USA
C) Sands Cotai Central, Macau, China

13. In what Indian state would you find the city of Agra, the site of the Taj Mahal?
A) Gujarat B) Rajasthan C) Uttar Pradesh

14. What is Morocco's currency?
A) Dinar B) Dirham C) Dollar

15. What is the smallest country in South America by land area?
A) Uruguay B) Guyana C) Suriname

16. In what US state is the annual Burning Man festival held?
A) Arizona B) Nevada C) Oregon

17. Roughly, how many bears are there living wild in Sweden?
A) 300 B) 3000 C) 30,000

18. In what country would you find the world's longest bridge?
A) USA B) China C) Japan

19. The Icelandic dish *hákarl* is made of what?
A) Fermented shark
B) Pickled cheese
C) Dried whale blubber

20. Perhaps the world's most famous extinct animal, the dodo was native to which island?
A) Madagascar B) Iceland C) Mauritius

Answers on p.107   Score

Quiz 61 **General Knowledge**

1. What is the current name of the US airport formerly known as Idlewild?

2. Port of Spain is the capital of which Caribbean country?
A) Cuba B) The Dominican Republic
C) Trinidad and Tobago

3. What dance was named in honour of Charles Lindbergh becoming the first person to fly non-stop between North America and the European mainland in 1927?

4. The Super Eagles is the nickname of which African country's football team?

5. In what country did the style of music known as bossa nova emerge in the 1950s? And, for a bonus point, what does 'bossa nova' mean?

6. What is this island?
A) Long Island, New York
B) Cyprus C) Great Britain

7. What large flightless bird, native to New Guinea and Australia, has a dagger-like claw on its second toe which can be up to 12.5 cm (5 in) long?

8. The Aventine, the Caelian, the Capitoline, the Esquiline, the Quirinal, the Viminal and the Palatine are better known as what?

9. Sumba, Lombok and Sulawesi are all islands belonging to what nation?

10. According to the Icelandic sagas, which Norse explorer established the first settlement on Greenland in the 10th century?
A) Erik the Red B) Harald Bluetooth
C) Olaf the Green

11. *Panthera onca* is the scientific name for which big cat?
A) Jaguar B) Leopard C) Snow leopard

12. What is the largest museum in the world?
A) Louvre, Paris
B) State Hermitage Museum, St Petersburg
C) National Museum of China, Beijing

13. The Skeleton Coast, littered with the remains of thousands of shipwrecks, lies on the edge of which African desert?

14. In what country would you find Lake Ladoga, the largest lake situated entirely in Europe?

15. *Tales of the City*, the 1978 novel by Armistead Maupin, and its eight sequels, are set in which US city?

16. The Hang Seng Index relates to a stock exchange located where?

17. Famed for its geysers and hot mud pools, in what country would you find the city of Rotorua?
A) Iceland B) New Zealand C) USA

18. What is the name of a ring-shaped coral reef enclosing a lagoon?

19. What is the capital of the United Arab Emirates?

20. Can you name the five US states that have a coast bordering the Pacific Ocean? You get a point for each.

Answers on p.107   Score

Quiz 62 **General Knowledge**

1. The Iguazú Falls lie on the border of which two South American countries?

2. The *Reinheitsgebot* is a German law relating to the production of which bar and restaurant staple?
A) Beer **B)** Sausages **C)** Pretzels

3. What sort of animal is a dik-dik, and where would you find it?

4. Completed in 2012, what Chinese dam spanning the Yangtze River is the world's largest power station?

5. Moctezuma II was the final ruler of which civilisation?
A) The Aztecs **B)** The Incas **C)** The Romans

6. What is the name of the island on which the Statue of Liberty stands?
A) Ellis Island **B)** Liberty Island
C) Statue Island

7. This is the outline of which country?

8. What is the name of the dust-filled wind that blows northwards from the Sahara into southern Europe?

9. A traditional food from Louisiana, what is a po'boy?
A) A spicy stew **B)** A sandwich
C) A meat salad

10. How long is Australia's Great Barrier Reef, the world's largest coral reef system?
A) 300 km (185 miles)
B) 1300 km (800 miles)
C) 2300 km (1430 miles)

11. Greenland is a territory of which European country?

12. What is the writing system – generally believed to be the world's first – made by pressing marks into wet clay, which was developed in Sumer in around 3400 BCE?
A) Cuneiform **B)** Hieroglyphs **C)** Runes

13. Mars regularly suffers from what meteorological phenomena?
A) Dust storms **B)** Snow showers
C) Tsunami

14. In which South American city can you browse for pointy hats and spell ingredients at the Witches' Market (El Mercado de las Brujas)?

15. Lake Balaton, Central Europe's largest lake, is located in which country?
A) Bulgaria **B)** Hungary **C)** Romania

16. In 1932, who became the first woman to fly solo across the Atlantic Ocean?

17. Studio Ghibli is an animation film studio based in which country?

18. In Turkey, what is a dolmus?
A) A shared taxi **B)** A vegetarian kebab
C) A small sailing boat

19. What is the largest city on New Zealand's South Island?

20. Can you name the five African countries that have coastlines on the Mediterranean Sea? You get a point for each.

Answers on p.107   Score

Quiz 63 **Food and Drink**

1. The letters DOCG on the label of a bottle of wine mean that it has been produced in which country?

2. The name of which spicy soup means 'pepper water' in the Tamil language?

3. In Iceland, if you ordered a plate of *lundi*, what would you be served?
A) Puffin B) Shark C) Lamb

4. What is the Japanese word for edible raw fish? (Careful now.)

5. The blue agave plant, which grows in central Mexico, is used to make what alcoholic drink?

6. In 1847, the confectioner Joseph Fry produced the first what?
A) Lollipop
B) Carbonated drink
C) Chocolate bar

7. What would you find placed inside a bottle of *ruou ran,* a Vietnamese drink made from rice wine?
A) A snake
B) A fermented egg
C) A plastic lucky charm

8. Hāngi is a traditional New Zealand method of cooking food using what?
A) A blowtorch
B) Hot rocks in an underground oven
C) Smoked cabbage tree leaves

9. From what French city does the fish stew known as bouillabaisse originate?

10. In what country would you find the Hunter Valley wine-growing region?

11. On what continent did tomatoes first grow in the wild?

12. What fruit is the main ingredient of the Puerto Rican dish *mofongo*?
A) Grapefruit B) Plantain C) Coconut

13. Gammel Dansk is an alcoholic drink from which country?
A) Denmark B) Netherlands C) Germany

14. What sort of creature is a fugu, eaten as a delicacy in Japan? It can be deadly if it's not expertly prepared so that the poisonous organs are removed.
A) Spider crab
B) Pufferfish
C) Asian giant hornet

15. Mole (pronounced 'mol-ay') is a spicy, Mexican sauce made from fruit, chilli peppers, spices and what other sweet ingredient?

16. What country does taleggio cheese come from?

17. Tia Maria is a Jamaican liqueur flavoured with what?

18. The lager San Miguel was first brewed in 1890 in what country?
A) Spain, B) Portugal C) The Philippines

19. The spicy meat casserole with an egg topping known as bobotie is from which African country?
A) Madagascar
B) Kenya
C) South Africa

20. Tapas are small snacks and dishes served in bars and restaurants in Spain. What does tapas literally mean?
A) Mini meals
B) Small plates
C) Lids

Answers on p.108   Score

Quiz 64 **General Knowledge**

1. In Tokyo, what are *oshiya*?
A) Fish market workers B) Sumo ticket sellers
C) Train pushers

2. The Caribbean island of Antigua forms part of a nation along with what other island?

3. In what European city was the Shakespeare play *Romeo and Juliet* set?

4. As of 2018, how many times have New Zealand won the Rugby Union World Cup?

5. What brightly coloured bird was considered sacred by many of the ancient civilisations of Mexico and Central America, including the Aztecs?

6. Where have most of the coronations of English monarchs taken place since 1066?
A) Winchester Cathedral
B) St Paul's Cathedral C) Westminster Abbey

7. What is the significance of the spacecraft *Vostok 1*?
A) It was used for the first manned space flight in history
B) It carried the first woman into space
C) It was the first spacecraft to reach Mars

8. Voodoo is a religion practised chiefly in which Caribbean country?

9. Counting Russia as part of Europe, what is Europe's longest river? And, for a bonus point, what is the longest European river outside of Russia?

10. In what South American country would you find the Cordillera Real mountains?

11. The travel and hotel comparison website Trivago was founded – and is still based – in which country?

12. What is the capital of Panama?

13. The Ashanti Empire occupied part of what modern African country from the 17th to the 20th century?

14. What world-famous museum opened in 1793 with a display of 537 paintings?

15. Rathambore, Sunderbans and Kanha are all national parks in which country?
A) China B) India C) Kenya

16. What is the name of the Australian port city immediately southwest of Perth?

17. Megalosaurus was the first dinosaur to be identified and given a proper scientific name in 1824. In what country was it discovered?
A) USA B) China C) England

18. Soca music originated on which Caribbean island?

19. In what country would you find this road of giant trees
A) Madagascar B) India C) France

20. Can you name the three complete countries found on the Iberian Peninsula? You get a point for each. And, for two bonus points, who do the two small remaining pieces of territory belong to?

Quiz 65 **General Knowledge**

1. What is the largest wild land mammal in South America?
A) The tapir B) The jaguar C) The elephant

2. In what country would you find the Great Sandy Desert?
A) Morocco B) Australia C) France

3. 'Except for the Marabar Caves – and they are twenty miles off – the city of Chandrapore presents nothing extraordinary' is the opening line to which classic novel set in Asia and first published in 1924?

4. The annual event at Cooper's Hill, Gloucestershire, England, involves competitors chasing what down a hillside?
A) A cheese B) A barrel C) A monkey

5. Which of these rivers flows into the Indian Ocean?
A) The Nile B) The Orinoco C) The Zambezi

6. In what city did Jesse Owens win four gold medals at the 1936 Olympic Games?

7. What famous confrontation took place in Tombstone, Arizona, on 26 October 1881?

8. Who was the first Roman emperor?
A) Julius Caesar B) Augustus C) Tiberius

9. The ancient city of Chichén Itzá in Mexico what built by which pre-Columbian people?

10. What is the capital of Finland?

11. What is the name of the building in Brussels consisting of nine giant metal spheres connected by tubes?

12. According to the last census in 2011, how many people live on Australia's Coral Sea Islands Territory?
A) 4 B) 4000 C) 40,000

13. What popular form of Japanese entertainment translates into English as 'empty orchestra'?

14. This statue in London's Bond Street, entitled *The Allies*, shows Winston Churchill talking to which US president?

15. Colón is a seaport next to which major waterway?
A) The Suez Canal B) The Panama Canal
C) The English Channel

16. Common, northern hairy-nosed, and southern hairy-nosed are the three recognised species of which southern hemisphere animal?

17. From 1883 to 1926, Monet lived in the village of Giverny in northern France. What type of plant from his garden often appeared in his paintings of this period?

18. What is the only planet in the solar system that's tilted over so it spins like a barrel, rather than like a top (as Earth does)?

19. After a 30-year-long civil war, the African state of Eritrea declared itself independent from which country in 1991?

20. Can you name the seven countries that contain parts of the Andes? You get a point for each.

Answers on p.108   Score [   ]

Quiz 66 **General Knowledge**

1. In what US state could you visit Grand Canyon National Park?

2. Which South American city has a name meaning 'River of January'?

3. If you were travelling by rail from Lime Street to New Street, what two English cities would you be travelling between?

4. What is the only continent where the leopard seal can be found living in the wild?
A) Antarctica B) Australia C) South America

5. How many astronauts have walked on the Moon?
A) 2 B) 12 C) 50

6. Nuuk is the capital and largest city of which Danish territory?

7. Which European language, spoken in a region encompassing parts of northern Spain and southwestern France, is known as Euskara by its native speakers?

8. The football team Santos play in which South American country?

9. Native to India and Southeast Asia, the red junglefowl is the closest relative of what common bird found right across the world?

10. Medellín is the second largest city in which country?

11. The name of which sausage derives from the Italian word for 'salted'?

12. Chilean writer Isabel Allende's debut novel was called *The House of the* what?
A) *Sun* B) *Birds* C) *Spirits*

13. Victoria is the capital of which island group in the Indian Ocean?

14. A popular Christmas plant in the USA and UK, the poinsettia originated where?
A) Canada B) Mexico C) Brazil

15. The Argentine Emilio Palma is known for what Antarctic-related feat?
A) He was the first person born on the continent (in 1978)
B) He was the first person to cross the continent barefooted
C) He discovered a new species of penguin there in 2003

16. A *Caganer*, a small figurine of a defecating man, is usually placed in the Christmas nativity scenes of what European region?

17. In what country would you see the strange mushroom-shaped rock formations know as fairy chimneys, shown here?

18. Which two countries claim to have invented the meringue-based dessert known as a pavlova? And, for a bonus point, who was the dessert named after?

19. On what day does France celebrate its national day, known as Bastille Day? And, for a bonus point, what event does it commemorate?

20. Can you name the four official languages of Singapore? You get a point for each.

©Albert Russ / Shutterstock

Answers on p.109   Score

Quiz 67 **Islands**

1. What is the largest island in the world?

2. What is the largest island in the Mediterranean Sea?
A) Sicily B) Malta C) Corfu

3. What is the name of the largest island in Japan where the capital, Tokyo, is located?
A) Hokkaido B) Honshu C) Madagascar

4. To what country does the Pacific island of Tahiti belong?
A) UK B) France C) USA

5. On which island was Napoleon Bonaparte born? And, for a bonus point, on which island did he die?

6. Steel drums were invented on which Caribbean island nation?
A) Jamaica B) Cuba C) Trinidad and Tobago

7. How many islands make up the archipelago of Fiji?
A) Between 1 and 100
B) Between 200 and 300
C) Over 300

8. Big Island is a common name for the largest island in what US archipelago?

9. The world's third largest island, Borneo, is divided between what three nations?

10. Which is the largest of the Balearic Islands: Mallorca, Menorca or Ibiza?

11. What is the name of the small island immediately south of Ibiza?

12. In what ocean would you find North Sentinel Island, part of the Andaman Islands, home to a small isolated tribe who have no contact with the outside world?
A) Indian B) Pacific C) Atlantic

13. To the nearest thousand, how many named islands are there in Indonesia?
A) 5000 B) 15,000 C) 50,000

14. Antananarivo is the capital of which Indian Ocean island nation, famed for its lemurs?

15. Christmas Island, the Ashmore and Cartier Islands, and the Cocos (Keeling) Islands are all island territories of which country?

16. What is the largest island in the Caribbean?
A) Jamaica B) Cuba C) Barbados

17. A Unesco World Heritage Site and major tourist destination, what is the name of the small island off the coast of Normandy which can be reached only via a narrow bridge (and which used to be cut off from the mainland completely at high tide)?

18. What is the capital of the Maldives?
A) Malé
B) Femalé
C) Maldives City

19. The bitter-orange flavoured liqueur curaçao is named after an island of the same name, which lies off the coast of which country?
A) Venezuela
B) USA
C) Spain

20. The 4,884 m (16,023 ft) Puncak Jaya, the world's tallest island mountain, can be found on what island?
A) New Guinea
B) Sicily
C) South Island, New Zealand

Answers on p.109   Score

Quiz 68 **General Knowledge**

1. The Wellcome Collection in London is a museum and library devoted to what?
A) Medical artefacts B) Home furnishings
C) Cinema

2. Mexico is the world's leading producer of which vegetable, a particular favourite with the modern generation?
A) Sweetcorn (maize) B) Avocados
C) Asparagus

3. Which Australian state has the largest population?
A) Queensland B) Victoria
C) New South Wales

4. What is the world's most biodiverse country, home to approximately 10% of all land-living species?

5. What is the name of the 4500 km (2800 mile) road that runs (albeit unpaved for long sections) through the desert between Lagos in Nigeria and Algiers in Algeria?

6. Built in the fifth century CE on top of a massive column of rock , the Sigiriya fortress is in which South Asian country?
A) India B) Bangladesh C) Sri Lanka

7. What is the name of the Brazilian martial art that combines fighting with elements of dancing and acrobatics?

8. In what French city was Joan of Arc burnt at the stake in 1431?
A) Orléans B) Paris C) Rouen

9. In what state is the US presidential retreat Camp David located?
A) California B) Maryland C) Alaska

10. What country has the largest amount of cork forest in the world?
A) Portugal B) India C) Brazil

11. Captain Matthew Webb, the first person to swim the English Channel unaided in 1875, died while trying to swim what other well-known body of water?
A) The Atlantic Ocean B) The Suez Canal
C) The rapids below Niagara Falls

12. During the annual festival of Naadam in Mongolia, competitors take part in what three traditional 'games of men'?
A) Cycling, swimming and running
B) Wrestling, horse racing and archery
C) Boxing, discus and pole vault

13. A picture of what features on the flag of Cambodia?
A) A Tiger B) The country's royal arms
C) Angkor Wat

14. The name of which European country means 'Black Mountain'?

15. Seen as one of England's finest examples of Georgian architecture, in what city would you find the Royal Crescent?

16. What links the sixth Olympic Games of 1916 with the twelfth Games of 1940?

17. What is name of the inland delta in Botswana that provides a home to a vast variety of wildlife, including elephants, lions, rhinos, hippos and crocodiles?

18. With an average of just 1.914 people per sq km, what is the least densely populated country on Earth?
A) Canada B) Finland C) Mongolia

19. What European country has three presidents, each with equal status?

20. Can you name the original Seven Wonders of the Ancient World? You get a point for each.

Quiz 69 **Ships and Boats**

1. What was the name of the ancient Greek galley, often used as a warship, powered by three banks of oars?
A) Bireme B) Trireme C) Catamaran

2. In what Scandinavian city would you find the Viking Ship Museum?
A) Gothenburg B) Oslo C) Copenhagen

3. What was the cruise liner sunk by the Germans in 1915 that led to the United States entering the First World War in 1917?

4. What was the ship that in 1620 sailed from Plymouth, England, to what would become Plymouth, Massachusetts, carrying 102 colonists known as the Pilgrim Fathers?

5. What is the Khufu ship?
A) A full-size ship buried at the foot of the Great Pyramid of Giza
B) A miniature ship discovered in the tomb of Tutankhamun
C) An Egyptian aircraft carrier

6. What was the name of the 1906 British battleship that was regarded as so powerful it became a synonym for all battleships?

7. What is the sci-fi-sounding name of the world's first nuclear-powered aircraft carrier, operated by the US from 1961 to 2012?
A) USS *Thunderbird* B) USS *Enterprise*
C) USS *Millennium Falcon*

8. On what ship did Sir Francis Drake sail all the way around the world from 1577 to 1580?
A) *Silver Beetle* B) *Bronze Lion* C) *Golden Hind*

9. What was the name of the Greenpeace ship sunk by French forces in New Zealand in 1987?

10. What was the ship that carried Captain Scott and his team on their ill-fated 1910–12 expedition to Antarctica?

11. What is the *Trieste*'s claim to fame?
A) It was the first deep-sea submersible to reach the bottom of the Mariana Trench, the deepest place on the surface of the Earth
B) It broke the record for the Atlantic crossing 12 times in the 19th century
C) It carried the crew that made the first recorded landing on Antarctica

12. What is the name of the 19th-century sailing ship that is on permanent display on the waterfront at Greenwich, London?

13. The world's oldest naval vessel still afloat, USS *Constitution*, was named in 1797 by which president?

14. Now a preserved museum ship in Portsmouth, England, HMS *Victory* was the flagship of which British naval hero at the Battle of Trafalgar?

15. What was the name of the raft on which the Norwegian explorer, Thor Heyerdahl, sailed for over 6900 km (4300 miles) from South America to Polynesia in 1947?

16. What was the name of the ship discovered in 1872 adrift and abandoned in the Atlantic Ocean off the Azores?

17. The long, paddled racing boats known as dragon boats originated in what country?

18. *Titanic* had two sister ships. *Britannic* was one; what was the name of the other?

19. What ship is best known for rescuing survivors of the *Titanic* after the disaster?
A) RMS *Carpathia* B) SS *Californian*
C) SS *Great Britain*

20. In what year was the movie *Titanic* starring Leonardo DiCaprio and Kate Winslet released?

Answers on p.110   Score

Quiz 70 General Knowledge

1. Roughly, what proportion of the world's population lives in the northern hemisphere?
A) 48% B) 68% C) 88%

2. The Ponte Vecchio is a famous bridge in which Italian city?
A) Rome B) Florence C) Turin

3. Consisting of a slight bow, performed with the palms pressed together, the *wâi* is a traditional greeting (or farewell) in which Asian country?

4. In what European city did the writer Mary Shelley first conceive of the story for her novel *Frankenstein*?
A) Paris B) Rome C) Geneva

5. In 2018, the African country of Swaziland changed its official name to what?
A) The Kingdom of Eswatini
B) The Gold Coast C) South East Africa

6. The 16th-century artist Doménikos Theotokópoulos is better known by which name, a reference to his place of birth?
A) Franco B) Amerigo C) El Greco

7. *Ghormeh sabzi*, *zereshk polo* and *faloodeh* are all dishes from which Middle Eastern country?

8. Tripoli is the capital of which North African country?

9. Which country's coat of arms (and football shirts) features a red-and-white chequerboard pattern?

10. In what Southeast Asian city could you see the Emerald Buddha?

11. The merengue is a music and dance that originated in which Caribbean country?

12. The Golden Boy of Pye Corner is a small gilded statue in London that commemorates the end of what event of 1666?

13. How tall is the Vaalserberg, the highest point in the otherwise rather low country of the Netherlands?
A) 32.4 m (106 ft) B) 322.4 m (1058 ft)
C) 3224 m (10,577 ft)

14. The novelist Mario Vargas Llosa is from what South American country?

15. The private house known as Fallingwater, built over a waterfall in rural Pennsylvania, was the work of which renowned 20th-century US architect?

16. Can you name the three museums in the South Kensington district of London that were established in the wake of (and largely with funds from) the Great Exhibition of 1851?

17. Pohutukawa trees, also known as Christmas trees (because of their bright red flowers) and iron trees, are found in what country?
A) South Africa B) Japan C) New Zealand

18. During the twice yearly equinoxes, a shadow is cast on the steps of the pyramid at Chichén Itzá resembling what animal?
A) A snake B) A bird C) A cat

19. Found in the rainforests of Sumatra, what is a *Rafflesia arnoldii*?
A) A plant that produces the world's largest flower
B) A plant that produces the world's smallest flower
C) A bird that looks like a flower

20. Can you name the original 13 colonies that formed the United States of America? You get a point for each.

Chapter 2

Answers

Answers

Quiz 31

1. Japan. The busiest of all is Shinjuku Station in Tokyo which processes a mind-boggling 1.26 billion people a year, or 3.45 million a day. The highest-ranking non-Japanese station is Gare du Nord in Paris, France, down in a lowly 24th.

2. A giant tortoise; specifically, a Pinta Island tortoise.

3. C) York. 'Jorvik' is the old Norse name for the city of York.

4. Barbados

5. India

6. The sandwich. John Montagu was the fourth Earl of Sandwich, who, according to legend, got his cooks to devise him a meal he could eat without leaving the gambling table.

7. Sam Neill

8. B) Museum of Modern Art, New York

9. The Moskva. It flows into the Oka, a tributary of the Volga.

10. Italy

11. A) Beaver

12. Masks

13. A) Disneyland

14. A) Mali

15. B) A fish (not a bird), which is usually dried and salted before being added to dishes.

16. It is set in ancient Egypt and was written by the Italian Giuseppe Verdi. Its first performance was in 1871.

17. C) Portugal

18. *Dulce de leche*

19. C) It's a small rodent-like marsupial native to Australia.

20. The Strip in Las Vegas

Quiz 32

1. B) Edinburgh, Scotland at 55.95°N, followed by C) Moscow at 55.75°N and then A) Vancouver at 49.28°N.

2. A) Make a mobile (cell) phone call. This was the first publicly observed call, made for the benefit of the reporters assembled for a press conference at the hotel.

3. The Dome of the Rock

4. A battle; it's a war dance.

5. The Rosetta Stone

6. Argentina. Bolivia. 1967.

7. Zebra

8. Denali. It means 'the high one' in the local Koyukon language.

9. B) Australia

10. C) A ghost or spirit

11. Sydney Opera House

12. A) A fish – it's a type of snailfish.

13. Thomas Cook

14. Cymru

15. B) Belarus

16. C) The Great Fire of London in 1666

17. The Arabian Desert

18. B) USA, which has over 250,000 km (155,000 miles) of track, followed by China with over 100,000 km (60,000 miles) – although this number is increasing all the time.

19. Hygge (pronounced 'hoo-ga')

20. Morocco, Algeria, Tunisia, Libya and Egypt

Quiz 33

1. The Urals

2. Haiti and the Dominican Republic

3. Colombia

4. Laos

5. Costa Rica

6. German (spoken by 63% of the population), French (spoken by 23%) and Italian (spoken by 8%).

7. Tunisia

8. B) A fungus – specifically a subterranean honey fungus that now covers an area 3.8 km (2.4 miles) across. For the most part, the only visible signs of it are the clumps of mushrooms – the fungus' fruiting bodies – that occasionally appear above ground.

9. B) Salzburg

10. A) Mexico

11. Bolivia and Paraguay

12. Japan. It's a 59 km (33 mile) rail tunnel that links the main island, Honshu, with the northern island of Hokkaido.

13. C) India. It's a 182 m (597 ft) statue of the Indian independence leader, Sardar Patel, in the state of Gujurat.

14. Caligula. He got the nickname as a child when he accompanied his father on military campaigns wearing a miniature soldier's outfit, complete with mini soldier's boots.

15. San Marino and the Vatican City

16. Chimpanzees

17. C) Rwanda

18. South America. It's spread across Brazil, Uruguay and Argentina.

19. Venice

20. Cathédrale Notre Dame de Paris

Answers

Quiz 34
Mountains

1. 1953
2. B) 8848 m (29,029 ft)
3. K2 in the Himalayas at 8611 m (28,251 ft).
4. Mauna Kea in Hawaii, which rises up 10,203 m (33,476 ft) from the sea bed. But only 4,207 m (13,802 ft) of it pokes above sea level.
5. Mt Elbrus at 5,642 m (18,510 ft)
6. Mont Blanc at 4810 m (15,781 ft)
7. Antarctica
8. B) Mt Whitney at 4,421 m (14,505 ft). It forms part of the Sierra Nevada in California.
9. The Atlas Mountains in Morocco.
10. Olympus Mons on Mars. It's a whopping 25,000 m (82,000 ft) high, or more than two and a half times the height of Mt Everest.
11. The Andes in South America at approximately 7000 km (4350 miles).
12. France and Spain
13. The Dolomites
14. Kilimanjaro
15. B) He completed the 'Seven Summits' – climbing the highest peak on each continent.
16. The Matterhorn
17. Mt Olympus
18. The Caucasus
19. C) Munros
20. Aconcagua in Argentina, at 6960.8 m (22,837 ft). Though the tallest anywhere outside Asia, it's just the 189th tallest on Earth.

Quiz 35

1. B) Wellington, New Zealand
2. C) Reykjavík, Iceland
3. B) Philadelphia
4. Whitby
5. Chile and Argentina
6. The Australian Open, the French Open, Wimbledon and the US Open
7. Monkeys. It's known as the Monkey Buffet Festival.
8. France, Spain and Morocco
9. Alexander the Great in the fourth century BCE (in around 332 BCE).
10. Venezuela, which means 'Little Venice' and was so named because it reminded the Spanish explorer Alonso de Ojeda of the European city.
11. The Great Ocean Road
12. The Brontë sisters: Anne, Charlotte and Emily
13. Cuba
14. C) Kendo. Aikido is an unarmed martial art, while ikebana is the Japanese art of flower arranging.
15. C) Boeing. It's where they make their planes.
16. Hogwarts School in the Harry Potter films
17. Georgia
18. A) Canada at 202,080 km (125,567 miles). Russia is fourth with 37,653 km (23,396 miles), while Australia is seventh with 25,760 km (16,000 miles).
19. A) Dakar, Senegal. At 49 m (161 ft), the African Renaissance Monument is taller than the Statue of Liberty.
20. London in 1908, 1948 and 2012

Quiz 36

1. A) USA with 175. Russia is second with 166 and Indonesia third with 139, although Indonesia is believed to have the greatest number of active volcanoes.
2. Ecuador, which is named after the Equator, the line of 0° latitude, which runs through it.
3. The French Revolution. It was completed in 1889 to mark the event's centenary.
4. The Gambia
5. Pakistan and Afghanistan
6. A) Gold Coast
7. B) Uranus
8. C) Greece
9. Vienna
10. B) The beautiful game
11. B) Hot dogs. In 2018, the reigning champion Joey Chestnut claimed the prize by downing 74 dogs and buns in ten minutes.
12. Carthage. The elephant march took place in 218 BCE during the Punic Wars (the Second Punic War to be exact).
13. Switzerland
14. C) Krakatoa is actually west of Java
15. Dublin
16. It was where the US conducted the first public test of a nuclear bomb in July 1946. Tests continued there until 1958.
17. The White House
18. Lake Eyre (officially Kati Thanda-Lake Eyre since 2012, to reflect the indigenous name used by the local Arabana people).
19. Argentina
20. Iowa, Ohio and Utah

Answers

Quiz 37

1. B) Hungary
2. A) Guatemala and Belize
3. Lagos
4. Guyana
5. A) Baht
6. A) A writing tablet
7. Skoda
8. B) Seven
9. Argon
10. *Star Wars*; it doubled as the Skywalker family home in several movies, including the first one.
11. Colorado
12. C) Emu
13. C) The Tay, which is also the longest river in Scotland.
14. B) Lebanon
15. A) Zurich
16. C) California
17. B) The Stasi
18. B) Australia. In 2016, it accounted for over 57% of global iron ore exports. Brazil was second with 25.1%, while South Africa was down in third with 4.3%.
19. The Alhambra
20. Norway, Finland, Estonia, Latvia, Lithuania, Poland, Belarus, Ukraine, Georgia, Azerbaijan, Kazakhstan, Mongolia, North Korea and China

Quiz 38 – Currencies and Money

1. Venezuela
2. Poland
3. B) Alexander the Great. The currency is called the lek, a diminutive form of 'Alexander' in Albanian.
4. C) Christopher Columbus. It's the colón, from the Spanish form of the explorer's name: Cristóbal Colón.
5. A) China, where knife money was an early form of currency.
6. B) Turkey. The coins were made of electrum, a naturally occurring alloy of gold and silver.
7. A buck
8. Pieces of eight. The Spanish dollar was a silver coin worth eight reales, with a large number '8' stamped onto it, hence its more piratey name.
9. South Africa
10. In China (where paper itself was invented) in the 8th century under the Tang Dynasty.
11. B) $100,000. They were printed in the 1930s and only used for transactions between government bodies, not by the general populace.
12. A) London, at a branch of Barclays Bank in Enfield.
13. Micronesia
14. C) Germany. The Berenberg Bank in Hamburg was founded in 1590.
15. B) Sweden. The Sveriges Riksbanks was founded in 1668.
16. C) Botswana
17. C) Wall Street. It's a bronze sculpture of a charging bull.
18. The yen
19. C) 100 billion, equivalent to 100 trillion according to modern counting methods.
20. A) France: franc B) Germany: mark C) Netherlands: guilder D) Spain: peseta E) Italy: lira F) Greece: drachma G) Portugal: escudo H) Finland: markka I) Ireland: pound (or punt) J) Slovenia: tolar

Quiz 39

1. C) *Across Asia on the Cheap*
2. Ukulele
3. A) Writing. He supposedly based the characters on the footprints of birds.
4. C) Japan. They're Japanese macaques, or snow monkeys, which famously like to keep warm by taking dips in the country's many volcanic hot springs.
5. A) Greece
6. Coventry. On the day of her ride, a proclamation was issued telling everyone to stay inside and shut their window so they wouldn't be able to see her. The only person to disobey was 'Peeping Thomas', who was blinded as a punishment for his voyeurism.
7. B) Indianapolis
8. Melbourne. Its former name was given to it by one of its founders, John Batman.
9. A) Thailand
10. El Salvador
11. Event horizon
12. B) Arc de Triomphe
13. Archipelago
14. B) Argentina
15. The Great Pyramid of Giza in Egypt, which was completed in c. 2560 BCE and at 146 m (481 ft) remained unsurpassed until the completion of Lincoln Cathedral in England in 1311 whose spire topped out at 160 m (525 ft). The spire was destroyed by a lightning strike in 1549.
16. A) Devon
17. A) Blue
18. B) A minibus used as a shared taxi, and often brightly patterned.

Answers

19. Austria. She was guillotined in 1793, along with her husband, during the French Revolution.

20. They are, going clockwise from the north: Denmark, Poland, Czech Republic, Austria, Switzerland, France, Luxembourg, Belgium and the Netherlands

Quiz 40

1. Howard Carter

2. New Zealand

3. A) Wyoming, with approximately 580,000 inhabitants.

4. B) Tokyo

5. Christ the Redeemer ('*Cristo Redentor*')

6. C) Geneva

7. The Roman Empire

8. B) Botswana

9. Glassmaking

10. Bicycle

11. William Shakespeare and Miguel Cervantes

12. The Crystal Palace. Built in Hyde Park, it was relocated to south London in 1854 where it burned down in 1936.

13. The thylacine, also known as the Tasmanian tiger (or wolf).

14. New York City

15. A) One third

16. B) Colombia. Its mines account for over 50% of all the emeralds produced.

17. The Terracotta Army, comprising more than 8000 clay soldiers built in the 3rd century BCE to guard China's first emperor, Qin Shi Huang, in the afterlife.

18. The Empire State Building, New York City

19. C) Singapore

20. Afghanistan, Kazakhstan, Kyrgyzstan, Pakistan, Tajikistan, Turkmenistan and Uzbekistan

Quiz 41

1. A) 13 – for the 13 original colonies that went on to form the United States of America.

2. B) Windermere

3. B) Turkey

4. Krakatoa

5. Moscow and Vladivostok for a total journey length of 9289 km (5772 miles).

6. C) Costa Rica

7. Alsace and Lorraine

8. A) Whales (southern right whales, to be specific).

9. Italy

10. B) Ethiopia

11. Australia

12. The snow leopard

13. A) São Tomé and Príncipe

14. C) Rivers. It has no permanent rivers, although short-lived temporary rivers do form after heavy rains. The island nation also doesn't have any mountains.

15. A) North Carolina

16. Phnom Penh

17. The Melbourne Cup, the country's most prestigious horse race.

18. C) India (146 million tonnes annually), with the USA second (93.5 million tonnes) and China third (45 million tonnes).

19. A) Glorious Revolution

20. A) .br is Brazil B) .ca is Canada C) .ch is Switzerland D) .cn is China E) .de is Germany F) .es is Spain G) .ke is Kenya H) .kr is South Korea I) .ma is Morocco J) .nz is New Zealand

Quiz 42
Film Locations

1. Rome

2. B) Oregon

3. Salzburg

4. C) Petra

5. Skopelos

6. Croatia

7. *Vertigo*

8. The Harry Potter films. The Hogwarts Express is shown riding across it.

9. *The Beach*

10. Chicago, where the characters played by Tony Curtis and Jack Lemmon witness a St Valentine's Day Massacre–style attack.

11. Costa Rica

12. Hawaii

13. Mumbai, India

14. Scotland, in Glencoe

15. Angel Falls in Venezuela

16. Ireland

17. Sicily

18. *When Harry Met Sally*

19. *The Martian*

20. A) Norway B) *Episode II: The Attack of the Clones*, where it was used for Theed, the capital of Naboo C) Ireland

Quiz 43

1. A) York

2. B) A small four-footed mammal related to the llama which lives in the upper reaches of the Andes.

3. Nitrogen

4. A) Hungary

5. Poland, as Maria Skłodowska in 1867. She later married the French scientist, Pierre Curie.

6. Chicago

7. Ferdinand Magellan. He

Answers

described it as 'pacific', meaning 'peaceful' because the water seemed so calm as he entered it with his small fleet. It wouldn't stay that way.

8. A) Ramses II who reigned for 66 years between 1279 and 1213 BCE.

9. A) Around 500 – fewer than you might think.

10. France and Switzerland, where it forms a tunnel with a 27 km (17 mile) circumference.

11. B) 1894

12. A) Rajasthan

13. B) Toronto

14. C) A dinosaur which, according to local legends, is supposed to inhabit the forests of the Congo. Descriptions are much like those of the Loch Ness Monster, and the pictures just as blurry.

15. C) US dollar

16. C) Australia

17. Frank Lloyd Wright

18. B) Wave Rock. It's a natural formation that's been turned into a wave-like shape by millions of years of weathering.

19. B) Tanzania. It forms a single block with the adjacent Masai Mara National Park in Kenya.

20. Manhattan, Brooklyn, Queens, The Bronx and Staten Island

Quiz 44

1. C) Bangladesh

2. C) Flowers

3. B) Bonn. The composer was born here in 1770. The house is now a museum.

4. C) Australia

5. A) Orinoco

6. C) Madagascar

7. C) Rose. It was adopted as the country's official flower in 1986.

8. India

9. London and Paris

10. Honolulu

11. B) A god who took the form of a feathered serpent. According to contemporary reports, the Aztecs believed the Spanish conquistador Hernan Cortez to be this god – something that greatly helped him in his attempts to subdue the empire.

12. C) Switzerland. It rises 744 m (2441 ft) along a short 1.7 km (1.05 miles) journey.

13. The Pantanal

14. Africa. It's in South Africa and is 610 m (2000 ft) high.

15. B) UK, in the English coastal resort of Southend-on-Sea. The pier stretches for 2158 m (7080 ft or 1.34 miles) out to sea.

16. B) Potato. Saag aloo is potato and spinach, aloo gobi is potato and cauliflower, while aloo gosht is potato and red meat.

17. B) Nigeria

18. A) Jamaica. It's next to James Bond Beach.

19. Petra in Jordan, the former capital of the Nabataean Kingdom. Despite his poetic musings, Burgon never actually visited the city.

20. George Washington, Thomas Jefferson, Abraham Lincoln and Theodore (not Franklin Delano) Roosevelt

Quiz 45

1. Tomatoes. It's known as La Tomatina. Around 20,000 people throw roughly 120,000 tonnes

(132,000 tons) of them. It gets quite messy.

2. Gold Coast

3. A) Cuba. Adult birds are just 5 cm (2 in) long, little bigger than a bumblebee.

4. Moa. The largest of these birds stood 3.6 m (12 ft) tall and weighed over 225 kg (500 lb).

5. B) Walk in space. He performed the first space walk in 1965.

6. Salmon – cured in salt, sugar and dill.

7. B) Addis Ababa, Ethiopia

8. 1912, on 15 April

9. C) Radio communication. In 1894, he invented the first transmitters and receivers for wireless telegraphy. The other two inventions were also by Italians: the battery by Alessandro Volta in 1800, and the espresso machine by Achille Gaggia in 1945.

10. Hyde Park

11. Maxim Gorky. The city was known as Gorky.

12. B) A pancake made with maize

13. B) Lotus

14. C) The Norwegian Roald Amundsen reached the pole on 14 December 1911, over four weeks ahead of the Brit Captain Scott, who died on the return journey. Robert Peary claimed to have been the first person to reach the North Pole in 1909, although doubts remain about his account.

15. A) Seattle

16. A) Algeria

17. B) Tennis. She won seven grand slam singles titles: three at Wimbledon and four

Answers

at the US Open.

18. The Southern Cross

19. A) 1903

20. New York City (8.6 million), Los Angeles (4 million), Chicago (2.7 million), Houston (2.3 million), Phoenix (1.63 million), Philadelphia (1.58 million), San Antonio (1.51 million), San Diego (1.42 million), Dallas (1.34 million) and San Jose (1.04 million)

Quiz 46
Museums

1. A) Liverpool, England

2. B) New York

3. C) Paris, France

4. A) London

5. B) Mexico City, Mexico

6. C) Washington DC

7. C) Canberra

8. A) Johannesburg

9. A) Athens, Greece

10. C) Tokyo, Japan

11. C) Tokyo, Japan

12. B) Madrid

13. A) Rio de Janeiro

14. C) Rome, Italy

15. B) Dakar, Senegal

16. B) Wellington

17. A) Bogotá, Colombia

18. C) Beijing

19. A) Port Louis, Mauritius

20. B) Santiago

Quiz 47

1. The Yangtze. At 6300 km (3915 miles), it's the third longest river in the world.

2. *Jaws*

3. Cape Town

4. C) Burj Khalifa, at 829.8 m (2722 ft).

5. B) Norway. To date, it has won

329 medals, followed by the United States in silver position with 282 and Germany claiming bronze with 228.

6. Peru, at Cordillera Rumi Cruz at the headwaters of the Mantaro River (according to a 2014 study, although there is still a degree of disagreement among the experts).

7. Glasgow

8. The wreck of the *Titanic*

9. The Tigris and the Euphrates. The word 'Mesopotamia' derives from the Greek for 'between two rivers'.

10. C) He was the final astronaut to reboard the Apollo 17 lunar module in 1972, making him the last human to walk on the Moon.

11. A representation of a human skull, usually made of sugar or clay.

12. London (Heathrow) and Los Angeles (International Airport)

13. C) Vanuatu

14. Pangaea

15. B) Osaka

16. The capybara

17. C) 60%

18. A) Belize

19. Haile Selassie I

20. Going west to east: France, Switzerland, Monaco, Italy, Germany, Liechtenstein, Austria, and Slovenia.

Quiz 48

1. A) Japan

2. South America

3. Portugal

4. Philadelphia, Pennsylvania. The 72 steps lead up to the front entrance of the Philadelphia Museum of Art.

5. A) 2061. It becomes visible from Earth every 74–79 years.

6. Adelaide

7. The Red Sea

8. A) Rotterdam, Netherlands

9. A) US Civil War

10. B) India

11. A) Common chimpanzee

12. A) Nile, in Egypt

13. Venus. The planet spins very slowly in retrograde – the opposite direction to Earth. It takes 243 Earth days to spin once on its axis, but just 224.65 Earth days to complete an orbit of the Sun, meaning that its day is actually longer than its year.

14. Seville

15. C) A reptile. It's a river dwelling crocodilian, related to crocodiles and alligators. It's critically endangered with fewer than 250 believed to exist in the wild.

16. South America

17. The Forbidden City. Formerly the royal palace of the Chinese emperors, it's now the Palace Museum.

18. Almonds

19. C) The bilby. Bilby numbers have declined significantly in recent years, partly as a result of competition with rabbits introduced to Australia in the 19th century.

20. A) Berlin Tegel is TXL, B) Chicago O'Hare is ORD, C) London Stansted is STN, D) Montréal–Pierre Elliott Trudeau is YUL, E) Newark Liberty is EWR, F) Rio de Janeiro–Antônio Carlos Jobim is GIG, G) Washington Dulles is IAD

Answers

Quiz 49 – The World of Books

1. C) Paul Theroux
2. *Cabaret*
3. A) New Orleans
4. C) Nigeria
5. Sir Edmund Hillary. It was his retelling of the first ascent of Mt Everest.
6. C) Edinburgh
7. Gabriel García Márquez
8. *To Kill a Mockingbird*
9. C) The October Revolution in Russia in 1917
10. B) *The God of Small Things*. *A Suitable Boy* is by Vikram Seth while *The Ministry of Utmost Happiness* is Roy's second novel, published 20 years after the first.
11. A) Paris, in *Down and Out in Paris and London* (1933).
12. B) *After Dark*
13. B) Bill Bryson
14. B) Bristol
15. C) St Petersburg
16. B) Cuba
17. C) The were all written (at least in part) while the author was in prison.
18. A) Jamaica
19. B) Mark Twain
20. A) Belgium
21. C) *The History of the Decline and Fall of the Roman Empire*
22. Stieg Larsson
23. C) India became an independent country
24. B) *The Brief Wondrous Life of Oscar Wao*
25. B) Iran

Quiz 50

1. A) 1932
2. Tokyo. It's also known as Tokyo International Airport.
3. Hugo Chávez
4. Jamaica
5. B) 900,000 approximately
6. B) The Danish King Harald Gormsson, famed for bringing his countries warring tribes together into a single kingdom
7. The Manneken Pis
8. A) 1858
9. The Proms. This annual series of orchestral concerts began in 1895.
10. C) New Zealand
11. A) Geothermal energy
12. The narwhal. Its tusk is actually an elongated tooth that pokes out of the left side of the animal's mouth. In the Middle Ages, these were often passed off as 'unicorn horns'.
13. Lake Titicaca
14. B) Southeast Asia
15. Romania
16. A) Kennedy Space Center
17. C) The Leaning Tower of Pisa. It started to tilt soon after it was begun, halting construction. When building work resumed, architects tried – unsuccessfully – to correct the tilt by building the upper floors with one side taller than the other.
18. A) Haiti
19. A) A mechanical model of the solar system
20. Going south to north: Democratic Republic of Congo, Tanzania, Burundi, Rwanda, Kenya, Uganda, South Sudan, Ethiopia, Sudan, Eritrea and Egypt.

Quiz 51

1. B) A Roman amphitheatre. Built in the first century CE, it is one of the best preserved of all Roman amphitheatres.
2. Yugoslavia. He was prime minister from 1944 to 1963 and President from 1953 until his death in 1980. The country was broken apart by a brutal civil war in the 1990s.
3. Basketball. He invented it using a peach basket and a soccer ball.
4. A) Antarctica, in the McMurdo Dry Valleys. It has a salt content of 44%, or around 12 times saltier than normal ocean water.
5. A) Autorickshaws
6. B) Around 7000
7. Otto von Bismarck
8. Turkey
9. President Herbert Hoover. It's the Hoover Dam.
10. Portugal
11. B) Thebes
12. Rio de Janeiro, Brazil
13. Mt Kosciuszko at 2,228 m (7,310 ft)
14. *Robinson Crusoe* by Daniel Defoe
15. B) Injera. *Wat* is a type of spicy Ethiopian stew, while *niter kibbeh* is clarified butter.
16. Colchester
17. Polynesia
18. None. Neither of the two planets closest to the Sun, Mercury and Venus, have moons.
19. The Statue of Liberty. It contains the famous lines: 'Give me your tired, your poor, Your huddled masses yearning to breathe free'.
20. A) Bridgetown = Barbados,

Answers

B) Tegucigalpa = Honduras, C) Quito = Ecuador. D) Asunción = Paraguay, E) Ljubljana = Slovenia, F) Tirana = Albania, G) Luanda = Angola, H) Dar es Salaam = Tanzania, I) Colombo = Sri Lanka, J) Port Moresby = Papua New Guinea

Quiz 52

1. Rum (specifically, white rum)
2. Jaipur, the capital of Rajasthan
3. Red polka dots
4. Africa, on the coasts of South Africa and Namibia. It's also known as the African penguin.
5. Japan. From 1603 to 1868, Japan was ruled by the Tokugawa Shogunate – essentially a military dictatorship – which instigated a strict isolationist foreign policy allowing only minimal trade with other countries at certain officially sanctioned areas. Commander Perry's arrival was instrumental in opening up Japan to the wider world and bringing about the restoration of imperial rule under Emperor Meiji.
6. Mascarpone is made from curds, while ricotta is made from whey – often leftover when making cheeses such as mascarpone.
7. Bats
8. B) The world's largest salt flat, encompassing an area of 10,582 sq km (4086 sq miles).
9. Australia
10. Granada
11. HMS *Beagle*
12. C) Arctic tern. Some birds make long meandering journeys of over 90,000 km (56,000 miles) between the Arctic

breeding grounds and Antarctic feeding sites, flapping all the way.
13. England and Wales. It is generally believed to have been built in the late 8th century by Offa, King of Mercia, to mark the border with the Welsh kingdom of Powys.
14. The Chrysler Building
15. 'La Marseillaise', which would become the French national anthem.
16. Twice, in 1978 and 1986
17. C) Malaysia and Indonesia
18. B) 2150, or almost ten times the number in Europe.
19. New York (John F Kennedy Airport) and Paris (Charles de Gaulle Airport)
20. *Enterprise* (the prototype), *Challenger* (destroyed during the lift-off stage in 1986), *Columbia* (disintegrated during re-entry in 2003), *Discovery*, *Atlantis* and *Endeavour* (built in 1991 to replace *Challenger*).

Quiz 53
Space

1. B) Methane
2. National Aeronautics and Space Administration
3. SpaceX
4. The Hubble Space Telescope. It was named after the US astronomer, Edwin Hubble (1889–1953).
5. B) Yellow dwarf or, more technically, a G-type main-sequence star.
6. Comets, which are usually made of a mixture of ice, dust and rock.
7. C) Skylab
8. B) 4.6 billion years ago

9. The Roman god of war
10. Galaxy
11. B) Russia
12. Venus, in 1961, by the Soviet probe *Venera 1*. It flew past the planet but radio contact with Earth was lost, so it didn't send back any data.
13. B) Water ice
14. C) 40,000 kph (25,000 mph). This is known as the escape velocity.
15. C) A rather roasting 15 million°C (27 million°F). The surface, however, is a comparatively chilly 5600°C (10,100°F).
16. Aurora (borealis in the north, australis in the south)
17. B) Sulphuric acid
18. The Goldilocks Zone
19. C) A planet orbiting a star in a solar system other than our own
20. B) From west to east. From directly above, the planet would appear to spin anticlockwise.

Quiz 54

1. A) Christmas Island, where there are an estimated 30 million crabs.
2. The Black Sea
3. England and Scotland. It was first played in 1879, and England currently have the upper hand with 70 wins to Scotland's 40.
4. Argentina
5. A) The Maldives
6. Archimedes, who lived his entire life in the Sicilian city of Syracuse, then a Greek colony. His impromptu streak was a result of his sudden realisation, while sat in the bath, that

Answers

it was possible to test the density of something by measuring how much water it displaced in a container.

7. B) Shark. It's the Greenland shark, which is believed to live up to 500 years. It doesn't even reach sexual maturity until it is 150 years old.

8. A) Italy, with 54. China is second with 53. Spain is third with 47, while Mexico is down in seventh with 34.

9. Los Angeles

10. The Moluccas or Maluku Islands

11. The Kentucky Derby. It's run over a short course of just one and a quarter miles (2 km) in Louisville, Kentucky.

12. Brussels, where it's also known, in French, as the Musée des instruments de musique and in Dutch as the Muziekinstrumentenmuseum.

13. B) Botswana

14. A) Olmecs. The Zapotecs and Toltecs were also Meso-American civilisations that flourished slightly later.

15. New Zealand

16. The Camargue

17. B) Venus. Although Mercury orbits closer to the Sun, it has almost no atmosphere to retain its heat, while Venus's thick carbon-dioxide-rich atmosphere traps the Sun's heat, raising temperatures to higher than 470°C (8880°F) – hot enough to melt lead.

18. B) Cuzco

19. The Great Rift Valley (or East African Rift)

20. A) O'Hare = Chicago, USA,

B) Dulles = Washington DC, USA, C) Ministro Pistarini = Buenos Aires, Argentina, D) Jorge Chávez = Lima, Peru, E) George Best = Belfast, Northern Ireland, F) John Lennon = Liverpool, England, G) Leonardo da Vinci = Rome, Italy, H) Jomo Kenyatta = Nairobi, Kenya, I) Narita = Tokyo, Japan, J) Kingsford Smith = Sydney, Australia

Quiz 55

1. B) Apollo 13. The mission was due to land on the Moon but ran into trouble when an oxygen tank exploded two days in. The crew were forced to navigate a new path which involved travelling round the far side of the Moon at a distance further than anyone has travelled before – or since.

2. B) A horse race – It takes place round the city's main square, the Piazzo del Campo.

3. Uruguay

4. The Hanging Gardens of Babylon

5. Venezuela. The phenomenon is also known as the 'Everlasting Storm'.

6. Africa. According to the UN, more than half of the global population growth currently taking place is happening there. If the rate continues at the same pace, then the continent's population will have more than doubled in forty years – from 1.03 billion in 2010 to 2.48 billion in 2050.

7. C) On floating islands made of reeds on Lake Titicaca

8. C) Turkey

9. The domestic chicken. At any

one time, there are an estimated 50 billion birds around the globe.

10. A sandwich containing pork, ham, mustard, cheese and pickles. Its name, which means 'midnight' apparently derives from its popularity as a late-night, post-partying snack.

11. London (Gatwick), UK, to Cape Town, South Africa.

12. C) USA and Canada at 8893 km (5525 miles) with B) Russia and Kazakhstan second at 6846 km (4254 miles) and A) Argentina and Chile third at 5300 km (3293 miles).

13. C) Krill. Despite its name, it doesn't feed on crabs at all.

14. Aberdeen

15. E) Horses. Of 254 animal-related deaths recorded in that period, 77 were caused by horses, 27 by dogs, 18 by kangaroos, 17 by sharks, and just 14 by snakes.

16. Skunk

17. Belgium

18. C) Russia. It stands for the Baikal Amur Mainline.

19. Australia. Dame Nellie Melba was one of the foremost sopranos of the late 19th and early 20th centuries.

20. A) Qantas = Australia, B) Gulf Air = Bahrain, C) Etihad = UAE, D) Lufthansa = Germany, E) El Al = Israel, F) Aer Lingus = Ireland, G) Air Astana = Kazakhstan, H) KLM = Netherlands, I) Tarom = Romania, J) Conviasa = Venezuela

Answers

Quiz 56
Landmarks

1. A) The Eiffel Tower. Lustig, from what is now the Czech Republic, was a notorious con man, not only selling the Eiffel Tower (twice), but also repeatedly convincing people to spend fortunes purchasing a 'Rumanian box' – a machine that could supposedly duplicate a note of any currency inserted into it. Handily, the machine took six hours to produce each copy, more than enough time for Lustig to make himself scarce before the deception was discovered.

2. B) London Bridge. This was one of the many successors to the original bridge, erected by the Romans in the first century CE. It was opened in 1831 and, when due to be replaced by a new structure in the late 1960s, dismantled and sold to the American businessman Robert P. McCulloch. McCulloch always knew what he was purchasing and, despite the persistent urban myth, never thought he was getting Tower Bridge.

3. The Maracanã. A match there between Brazil and Uruguay at the 1950 World Cup was attended by 199,854 people – still a record for a sporting event in an enclosed stadium.

4. C) The Empire State Building. The silent film, entitled *Empire*, consists of a single stationary shot of the building, the highlight being when the lights turn on as night falls.

5. It's the Burj Khalifa, Dubai, United Arab Emirates, the tallest building in the world.

6. St Peter's Basilica

7. B) Queensland

8. B) The bell

9. California

10. The Battle of Stalingrad (1942–43). It stands in Volgograd (the modern name for Stalingrad), and is 85 m (279 ft) tall.

11. C) The Taj Mahal

12. C) The Luxor. The light measures a not inconsiderable 42.3 billion candela – the standard SI unit of luminous intensity.

13. A) St Basil's Cathedral

14. Mt Kilimanjaro, Tanzania

15. C) Auckland, New Zealand

16. A) Neuschwanstein Castle

17. B) Tennessee

18. Monument Valley

19. C) Istanbul, formerly Constantinople, which was then the capital of the Eastern Roman Empire. The building began life as a cathedral, was later changed into a mosque, and is now a museum.

20. Machu Picchu

21. B) 14 years, from 1869 to 1884.

22. Brandenburg Gate, Berlin, Germany

23. Angkor Wat

24. B) Athena

25. B) It was relocated to higher ground to avoid being submerged by the lake created by the newly built Aswan Dam.

Quiz 57

1. C) Maine

2. B) Málaga

3. Verona, Italy

4. Russia. Kaliningrad is a Russian exclave, lying between Poland and Lithuania.

5. Captain James Cook

6. Nairobi, Kenya

7. The passenger pigeon. The last known individual, a female called Martha, died in Cincinnati Zoo in 1914.

8. C) A small carved ornament used for attaching objects to the sash of a kimono. They were developed because traditional kimonos don't have pockets. Netsuke are now used more as ornaments than functional objects.

9. Neptune

10. Tulips. It is generally regarded as the first speculative bubble. There have been plenty since – and all have ultimately popped.

11. Australia

12. Vienna, Austria

13. B) 2008

14. The saltwater (or estuarine) crocodile

15. Ghana

16. B) Amsterdam in 1602. It was established by the Dutch East India Company to help finance its growing trading empire – which involved, among other things, the importation of tulip bulbs.

17. Chile

18. Beetroot

19. Washington DC is the site of 17 Smithsonian museums, 11 of which are located on the National Mall.

Answers

20. Greece, Bulgaria, Georgia, Armenia, Azerbaijan, Iran, Iraq and Syria

Quiz 58
1. B) 54
2. Suriname. It was formerly a Dutch colony.
3. Laos
4. C) The maximum depth the ship may be safely immersed in water
5. B) The boundary between Earth's atmosphere and outer space. It was set by the Hungarian-American physicist Theodore von Kármán at 100 km (62 miles) above Earth's sea level.
6. Liechtenstein
7. Australia. The service runs between Adelaide on the country's southern coast and Darwin on its northern coast.
8. Salisbury
9. The Superbowl
10. A) The Hercules moth, with wings of 300 sq cm (46 sq inches), is found in New Guinea and Northern Australia. The Queen Alexandra is the biggest butterfly, while the Titan beetle is the biggest species of beetle.
11. Portugal
12. New York
13. C) Southeast Asia. They're divided between four countries: Malaysia, Indonesia, Brunei and East Timor.
14. The Leaning Tower of Pisa
15. A) A low grey (or white) blanket
16. C) Cretaceous
17. A) Architecture

18. A) The Andean condor, which has a wingspan up to 3.3 m (10 ft 10 in)
19. Fiji
20. 1. France (82.6 million visitors), 2. USA (77.5 million), 3. Spain (75.6 million), 4. China (59.3 million), 5. Italy (52.4 million), 6. Turkey (39.5 million), 7. UK (35.8 million), 8. Germany (35.6 million), 9. Mexico (35 million), 10. Thailand (32.6 million)

Quiz 59
Transport
1. B) Indonesia
2. South Africa. It travels between Pretoria and Cape Town.
3. C) San Marino. The tiny republic enclosed within Italy is the only country to officially have more cars than people, at 1263 motor vehicles per 1000 people. The USA is second with 910 per 1000, and Monaco third with 899 per person.
4. B) Argentina. *El Tren del Fin del Mundo*, or the Southern Fuegian Railway, operates in Tierra del Fuego province. It was originally built in 1909 to ferry prisoners to Ushuaia Prison, but is now a heritage line.
5. B) Royal Caribbean International. *The Harmony of the Seas* is currently the world's largest cruise liner.
6. B) It's the heaviest moving land vehicle ever made. The Bagger 293 is giant bucket wheel excavator weighing around 12,800 tonnes (14,200 tons).
7. A) London. The first

passengers were transported in gas-lit carriages pulled by steam locomotives. It must have been startlingly smelly and dirty – but also popular, carrying an incredible 38,000 people on its first day of operation.
8. Howard Hughes. Properly named the *Hughes H-4 Hercules*, the flying boat made just a single test flight in 1947.
9. C) 1228 kph (763 mph), making it the first car to break the sound barrier. The 'SSC' stands for 'super sonic car'.
10. A) France. The balloon was made by the Montgolfier brothers, Joseph-Michel and Jacques-Étienne using taffeta covered with an alum varnish (to make it fireproof).
11. Bullet trains
12. *Voyager 1*. Launched in 1977, in 2012 it became the first spacecraft to exit the solar system and enter interstellar space.
13. A) The steam locomotive. His first contraption hauled a train at the Penydarren Ironworks in Wales in 1804.
14. A) The American War of Independence. Named the *Turtle*, the hand-operated craft was designed to secretly attach explosives to British ships (although all its attempts to do so failed).
15. Karl Benz of Germany. His Benz Patent-Motorwagen of 1885 is generally accepted to be the first automobile.
16. B) *Mallard*
17. The Wright Brothers performed the first powered

Answers

flight in an aircraft.

18. C) 7.3 km (4.53 miles).
Made up of eight locomotives
and 692 wagons, it carried
82,000 tonnes (90,000 tons)
of iron ore along a 275 km
(170 mile) stretch of track, from
a mine to Port Hedland on the
coast of Western Australia on
21 June 2001 – and was
controlled by just a single driver.
The YouTube video showing it
going past the camera lasts
over eight minutes.

19. B) Boeing 747 'Jumbo Jet'

20. Longitude. His marine
chronometer, or sea clock,
kept such accurate time –
even when being buffeted by
the motion of the waves –
that sailors could use it to
plot their routes precisely.

21. Chattanooga Choo Choo

22. A) Hartsfield-Jackson is
the busiest, processing over
104 million passengers annually,
followed by Beijing with
96 million and Dubai with
88 million.

23. C) France

24. A) The Qatar Airways flight
from Auckland, New Zealand to
Doha Qatar covers 14,536 km
(9032 miles) and takes
18 hours 5 minutes. Second is
the Qantas flight from Perth,
Australia to London, UK, which
covers 14,500 km (9010 miles)
and takes 17 hours 20 minutes,
followed by the Emirates flight
from Auckland to Dubai, which
covers 14,200 km (8824 miles)
and lasts 17 hours 5 minutes.

25. i) A = Austria, ii) AUS =
Australia, iii) BR = Brazil,

iv) C = Cuba, v) CDN = Canada,
vi) CI = Ivory Coast (Côte
d'Ivoire), vii) E = Spain,
viii) FJI = Fiji, ix) GB: United
Kingdom, x) J = Japan,
xi) NZ = New Zealand,
xii) RA = Argentina (República
Argentina), xiii) ROK = South
Korea, xiv) USA = USA,
xv) ZA = South Africa

Quiz 60

1. A) Mali
2. B) Tasman Sea
3. C) India
4. C) Subway
5. A) Mexico
6. C) Algeria
7. B) Nigeria
8. A) Finland
9. C) 16,000
10. B) 69
11. C) Lazio
12. A) First World Hotel,
Malaysia, with 7351 rooms.
The Venetian (along with the
adjoining complex The Palazzo)
is second with 7117. Two further
Las Vegas hotels take the third
and fourth spots (MGM Grand
and CityCenter), while
the Sands Cotai is fifth with
6000 rooms.
13. C) Uttar Pradesh
14. B) Dirham
15. C) Suriname
16. B) Nevada
17. B) 3000
18. B) China. It's the Danyang–
Kunshan Grand Bridge, which
carries part of the Beijing-
Shanghai Railway and stretches
for 165 km (102.4 miles).
19. A) Fermented shark
20. C) Mauritius

Quiz 61

1. John F. Kennedy International
Airport, which serves New
York City.
2. C) Trinidad and Tobago
3. The Lindy Hop
4. Nigeria
5. Brazil. 'Bossa nova' translates
as 'new wave'.
6. B) Cyprus
7. Cassowary
8. The seven hills of Rome
9. Indonesia
10. A) Erik the Red
11. A) Jaguar
12. A) The Louvre, with 72,735 sq
metres (782,910 sq ft) of gallery
space. The State Hermitage is
second with 66,842 sq metres
(719,840 sq ft), while the
National Museum of China
is third with 65,000 sq metres
(700,000 sq ft).
13. The Namib Desert
14. Russia
15. San Francisco
16. Hong Kong
17. B) New Zealand
18. Atoll. It's formed when a
volcano sinks into the sea,
leaving behind the fringing
ring of coral.
19. Abu Dhabi
20. From north to south
on the mainland: Alaska,
Washington, Oregon, California,
and then out in the Pacific
Ocean itself, Hawaii.

Quiz 62

1. Brazil and Argentina
2. A) Beer. It's the 'Beer Purity
Law', passed in 1516 and still in
effect, which states that beer can
only be made using hops, barley,

- Lonely Planet's Ultimate Travel Quiz Book -

Answers

water and yeast.

3. It's a small antelope native to southern Africa.

4. The Three Gorges Dam

5. A) The Aztecs. He was killed during the Spanish conquest of the Aztec Empire in the 16th century.

6. B) Liberty Island

7. France

8. Sirocco

9. B) A sandwich, usually made using a baguette-like New Orleans French roll.

10. C) 2300 km (1430 miles)

11. Denmark

12. A) Cuneiform

13. A) Dust storms

14. La Paz, Bolivia. You can also pick up some unusual ingredients, such as dried llama foetuses (for luck, of course).

15. B) Hungary

16. Amelia Earhart. The American aviator became a global celebrity, but disappeared during an attempt to fly around the world in 1937. What became of her remains a mystery.

17. Japan. It's produced several highly successful anime feature films, including the 2011 worldwide hit *Spirited Away*.

18. A) A shared taxi

19. Christchurch

20. Morocco, Algeria, Tunisia, Libya and Egypt

Quiz 63
Food and Drink

1. Italy. The letters stand for *Denominazione di Origine Controllata e Garantita*, the highest classification for Italian wines.

2. Mulligatawny, from the words 'milagu' meaning 'pepper' and 'tanni' meaning water.

3. A) Puffin

4. Sashimi (sushi, with which it's often confused, is actually rice).

5. Tequila

6. C) Chocolate bar

7. A) The body (and sometimes the venom and blood) of a snake.

8. B) Hot rocks in an underground oven

9. Marseille

10. Australia

11. South America

12. B) Plantain

13. A) Denmark

14. B) Pufferfish (or blowfish)

15. Chocolate

16. Italy

17. Coffee

18. C) The Philippines

19. C) South Africa

20. C) Lids. According to one theory, the name derives from the practice of placing the dishes on top of bar drinks to protect them from flies.

Quiz 64

1. C) Train pushers – they work during the rush hour to push as many people into each carriage as possible.

2. Barbuda

3. Verona, Italy

4. Three times, the most of any nation.

5. The quetzal

6. C) Westminster Abbey

7. A) It was used for the first manned space flight in history, launching Yuri Gagarin into orbit (and the history books) in 1961.

8. Haiti

9. The Volga. The Danube.

10. Bolivia

11. Germany

12. Panama City

13. Ghana

14. The Louvre in Paris

15. B) India. All three have populations of tigers.

16. Fremantle

17. C) England

18. Trinidad and Tobago

19. A) Madagascar. It's the Avenue of Baobabs.

20. Spain, Portugal and Andorra are the three countries. A small area of France occupies the peninsula's northeast edge, while Gibraltar at its southern tip is a British Overseas Territory.

Quiz 65

1. A) The tapir (the lowland, or South American, tapir to be specific).

2. B) Australia. It's the country's second largest desert.

3. *A Passage to India* by E. M. Forster

4. A) A Cheese

5. C) The Zambezi. The Nile flows into the Mediterranean Sea while the Orinoco flows into the Atlantic Ocean.

6. Berlin. The games were staged by the Nazi regime – Owens' feats somewhat undermining Hitler's theories of German physical superiority.

7. The Gunfight at the OK Corral

8. B) Augustus

9. The Maya

10. Helsinki

- 108 -

Answers

11. The Atomium. It was built for the 1958 World's Fair and is now a museum.

12. A) Just four, who operate the weather monitoring station there.

13. Karaoke

14. Franklin Delano Roosevelt

15. B) The Panama Canal

16. Wombat

17. Waterlillies

18. Uranus

19. Ethiopia

20. Venezuela, Colombia, Ecuador, Peru, Bolivia, Chile and Argentina

Quiz 66

1. Arizona

2. Rio de Janeiro – the irony being that the city doesn't have a river, but lies next to a large bay.

3. Liverpool and Birmingham

4. A) Antarctica

5. B) Twelve men have walked on the Moon, the last in 1972. No one has been back since.

6. Greenland

7. Basque – the language is unrelated to any other language.

8. Brazil

9. The domestic chicken, which is believed to be descended from red junglefowl that were domesticated around 5000 years ago.

10. Colombia

11. Salami

12. C) Spirits

13. The Seychelles

14. B) Mexico. It's named after the man who introduced it to the US in 1825, Joel Roberts Poinsett, the first US minister to Mexico.

15. A) He was the first person

born on the continent (in 1978)

16. Catalonia in Spain

17. Turkey

18. Australia and New Zealand. It was named after the Russian Anna Pavlova, one of the leading ballerinas of the early 20th century, who toured both countries in the 1920s.

19. 14 July. It commemorates the storming of the Bastille (a prison in Paris), the event that kick-started the French Revolution.

20. English, Mandarin, Malay and Tamil

Quiz 67
Islands

1. Greenland. Australia is larger but is technically a continent.

2. A) Sicily

3. B) Honshu

4. B) France

5. He was born on Corsica, and died on St Helena.

6. C) Trinidad and Tobago

7. C) Over 300

8. Hawaii

9. Malaysia, Indonesia and Brunei

10. Mallorca

11. Formentera

12. B) Pacific. Officially part of India, the island is not controlled directly by the Indian government, who instead have a policy of preserving the island's (and tribe's) isolation, so as to protect them from contracting diseases to which they may have no immunity. It is illegal for anyone to visit the islands. People who have done so have occasionally been attacked and

even killed, as happened to the American missionary John Chau in 2018. The Indian government does not prosecute the islanders for these killings.

13. B) 15,000 – 14,752 is the latest UN-accepted figure, although Indonesia is doing a recount, so this may well rise.

14. Madagascar

15. Australia

16. B) Cuba

17. Mont St-Michel

18. A) Malé

19. A) Venezuela

20. A) New Guinea, in Indonesia

Quiz 68

1. A) Medical artefacts

2. B) Avocados

3. C) New South Wales with 7.48 million people. Victoria is second with 5.9 million and Queensland is third with 4.7 million.

4. Brazil

5. The Trans-Sahara Highway

6. C) Sri Lanka

7. Capoeira

8. C) Rouen

9. B) Maryland

10. A) Portugal. It's home to around 30% of the world's cork trees.

11. C) The rapids below Niagara Falls

12. B) Wrestling, horse racing and archery

13. C) Angkor Wat

14. Montenegro

15. Bath

16. They were both cancelled owing to the outbreak of war. The first was to have been staged in Berlin (and was 20 years later),

Answers

while the second was to have been staged in Tokyo (and was in 1964, and will be again in 2020).

17. The Okavango Delta

18. C) Mongolia

19. Bosnia and Hercegovina: one Serb, one Croat and one Bosniak to ensure fair representation.

20. 1. The Great Pyramid of Giza, 2. The Hanging Gardens of Babylon, 3. The Colossus of Rhodes, 4. The Lighthouse (or Pharos) of Alexandria, 5. The Temple of Artemis at Ephesus, 6. The Mausoleum of Harlicarnassus, 7. The Statue of Zeus at Olympia

Quiz 69
Ships and Boats

1. B) Trireme

2. B) Oslo

3. *Lusitania*

4. *Mayflower*

5. A) A full-size ship buried at the foot of the Great Pyramid of Giza, for use by the pharaoh in the afterlife.

6. HMS *Dreadnought*

7. B) USS *Enterprise*

8. C) *Golden Hind*

9. *Rainbow Warrior*. The ship had been on its way to protest (and try to disrupt) a French nuclear test.

10. *Terra Nova*

11. A) In 1960, it became the first deep-sea submersible to reach the bottom of the Mariana Trench in the Pacific Ocean, the deepest place on the surface of the Earth.

12. *Cutty Sark*. It's a tea clipper built in 1869 and one of the fastest ships of its day. It's now

back on display following a devastating fire in 2007.

13. George Washington

14. Lord Nelson

15. *Kon-Tiki*

16. *Mary Celeste*. Why her crew had suddenly abandoned a perfectly seaworthy ship remains unexplained to this day.

17. China

18. *Olympic*

19. A) RMS *Carpathia*. The *Californian* was widely condemned for not responding to the tragedy, despite being the closest ship.

20. A) 1997

Quiz 70

1. C) 88%, or almost nine out of every ten people.

2. B) Florence

3. Thailand

4. C) Geneva, Switzerland. Much of the novel is also set there.

5. A) The Kingdom of Eswatini

6. C) El Greco ('The Greek'). He was born in Crete in 1541.

7. Iran. *Ghormeh sabzi* is a herb stew, *zereshk polo* is chicken, barberries and rice, while *faloodeh* is a type of sorbet flavoured with rose water.

8. Libya

9. Croatia

10. Bangkok., Thailand. It's actually made of jade rather than emerald.

11. Dominican Republic

12. The Great Fire of London

13. B) Just 322.4 m (1058 ft)

14. Peru

15. Frank Lloyd Wright

16. The Natural History Museum, the Science Museum, and the

Victoria and Albert Museum (or V&A)

17. C) New Zealand

18. A) A snake

19. A) A plant that produces the world's largest flower (and a putrid smell of decaying flesh).

20. Connecticut, Delaware, Georgia, Maryland, Massachusetts, New Hampshire, New Jersey, New York, North Carolina, Pennsylvania, Rhode Island, South Carolina and Virginia

Chapter 3
Explorer
(Hard)

Quiz 71 **Lonely Planet**

Can you work out the destination from its description by a Lonely Planet
writer? It could be a country or a city or a region... or anywhere really.
To help you, we've provided the first letter of each answer.

1. What 'L' is this?
'After Cairo, this sprawling metropolis is the
second-driest world capital, rising above a
long coastline of crumbling cliffs. To enjoy it,
climb on the wave of chaos that spans high-
rise condos built alongside pre-Columbian
temples, and fast Pacific breakers rolling
toward noisy traffic snarls.'

2. What 'O' is this?
'The closest thing to Eden left on the planet.
Amid the sandy thorn-scrub of the Kalahari
Desert, its 15,000 sq km of champagne-
coloured rivers, papyrus-choked reed beds
and lily-covered lagoons represent one of the
largest wetland wildernesses in the world.'

3. What 'N'? is this?
'A curtain of fluttering prayer flags... A
trekkers' paradise combining mountain
views, golden temples, charming hill villages
and jungle wildlife watching.'

4. What 'E' is this?
'Few areas in the world possess a more
mystical pull than this tiny speck of land.
Endowed with the most logic-defying
statues on the planet, it emanates a
magnetic, mysterious vibe.'

5. What 'L'? is this?
'An oasis of indulgence dazzling in the
desert, promising excitement, entertainment,
fortune and fame. Seeing is believing.'

6. What 'Y' is this?
'No other city in northern England says
'medieval' quite like here... A magnificent
circuit of 13th-century walls encloses a
medieval spider's web of narrow streets. At its
heart lies the immense, awe-inspiring Minster.'

7. What 'P' is this?
'Monument-lined boulevards, museums,
classical bistros and boutiques... enhanced
by a new wave of multimedia galleries,
creative wine bars, design shops and tech
start-ups.'

8. What 'L' is this?
'A pulsating powerhouse... With burgeoning
tech industries, posh restaurants and clubs,
and an exploding arts scene, this megacity is
the face of modern Africa.'

9. What 'A' is this?
'No place on Earth compares to this vast
white wilderness of elemental forces: snow,
ice, water, rock.'

10. What 'N' is this?
'Get ready for mammoth national parks,
dynamic culture, and world-class surfing
and skiing. Filling in the gaps are the forests,
mountains, lakes, beaches and fiords that
have made this one of the best hiking (locals
call it 'tramping') destinations on the planet.'

11. What 'E' is this?
'This is not just a wetland, or a swamp, or a
lake, or a river, or a prairie, or a grassland – it
is all of the above, twisted together into a
series of soft horizons, long vistas, sunsets
that stretch across your entire field of vision.'

12. What 'T' is this?
'Neon-lit streetscapes look like a sci-fi film
set, pushing the boundaries of what's possible
on densely populated, earthquake-prone land,
adding ever taller, sleeker structures. Look out
over the city at night to see it blinking like the
control panel of a starship, stretching all the
way to the horizon.'

Answers on p.144   Score

Quiz 72 **General Knowledge**

1. In 1914, the world's first set of electric traffic lights was installed in which city?
A) London, England **B)** Paris, France **C)** Cleveland, Ohio, USA

2. The tiny archipelago of Tristan da Cunha is the most remote inhabited place on Earth, lying in the Atlantic Ocean 2000 km (1243 miles) from St Helena, the nearest inhabited island. What is the nearest mainland country, around 2400 km (1490 miles) away?
A) Argentina **B)** Morocco **C)** South Africa

3. The world's tallest human-made fountain is in which country?
A) USA **B)** Saudi Arabia **C)** Australia

4. In what US city is the headquarters of NASA located?
A) Houston **B)** Washington DC **C)** Miami

5. Reinhold Messner was the first person to climb Mt Everest alone, and the first person to climb all 14 mountains over 8000 m (26,200 ft). What country is he from?
A) Germany **B)** Switzerland **C)** Italy

6. Tollund man, a 2200-year-old 'bog body' (a corpse naturally mummified in peat) was discovered in which European country?
A) Ireland **B)** Denmark **C)** Finland

7. A *hanbok* is a traditional dress from which country?
A) Norway **B)** Mali **C)** South Korea

8. What is the name of the New Zealand scientist who first 'split the atom' in 1917?

9. The *Casa Rosada*, or 'Pink House', is the home and executive mansion of the president of which South American country?

10. *Sagarmatha* and *Chomolunga* are two lesser-known names for what giant landmark?

11. The largest open-air market in Africa is located in what city?
A) Addis Ababa, Ethiopia **B)** Cairo, Egypt **C)** Cape Town, South Africa

12. Kiiking, an extreme form of swinging, in which the aim is to make the swing do a 360° loop-the-loop, was invented where?
A) USA **B)** Slovenia **C)** Estonia

13. Lying 258 m (846 ft) below sea level, which ancient Middle Eastern city is the lowest in the world?
A) Baghdad, Iraq **B)** Muscat, Oman **C)** Jericho, Palestinian Territories

14. What are the only two places where giant tortoises are found in the wild?

15. When did the African country of Benin gain its independence, and from whom?

16. Bactrian camels originated in what country?
A) Mongolia **B)** Kazakhstan **C)** Afghanistan

17. What was the American playwright Tennessee Williams' real first name?
A) Thomas **B)** Tenacious **C)** Tennessee

18. In what South American country would you find the Middle of the World Monument (Monumento a la Mitad del Mundo) located directly on the Equator?

19. Norfolk Island is a small territory belonging to what country?
A) UK **B)** USA **C)** Australia

20. Uzbekistan is the only country in Asia that is double-landlocked (surrounded by countries that are also landlocked). Can you name the five landlocked countries that surround it? You get a point for each. Clue: they all end in 'stan'.

Answers on p.144   Score

Quiz 73 **General Knowledge**

1. What are the two languages of government in India? And, for a bonus point, how many official languages are there in India?

2. The name of which South American country is derived from the Latin word for silver?

3. What was the name of the treaty that officially ended the First World War?

4. What is the mistral?
A) A lighthouse B) A wind C) A desert

5. What is the brightest star in the night sky?

6. The eruption of which Indonesian volcano in 1815 is believed to be the most destructive in recorded history?

7. The north face of which Swiss mountain is considered so dangerous to climb that it has been given the German nickname Mordwand (meaning 'murder wall').

8. The kakapo is an extremely rare species of flightless parrot from which country?

9. Windhoek is the capital of which southern African country?

10. In what year did India gain independence from the United Kingdom?
A) 1907 B) 1947 C) 1967

11. The island nation of Trinidad and Tobago lies off the coast of which South American country?

12. Who was the first German to win the men's singles tennis title at Wimbledon?

13. Today, the former city of Tsaritsyn is known as Volgograd, but by what name was it known between 1925 and 1961?

14. Mr Chicken was the last private resident of which famous London address?

15. Mines in the state of South Australia, particularly those around the town of Coober Pedy, are the source of over 80% of the world's supply of which gemstone?

16. In 1946, which country's leader issued a statement renouncing his divinity?

17. Born in England around 1680 and killed off the coast of North Carolina in 1718, following a life spent at largely sea, Edward Teach is better known to history as who?

18. Espirito Santo is a state in which South American country?

19. In what country would you see goat-filled argan trees, such as this one?

20. Match the country to the national dish. You get a point for each.
Countries: A) Austria B) Albania C) Barbados D) Canada E) Ethiopia F) Finland G) France H) Georgia I) Jamaica J) Lebanon K) Peru L) South Korea

National dishes: kimchi, kibbeh, *khachapuri, karjalanpaisti,* poutine, *tavë kosi*, Wiener schnitzel, cou-cou and flying fish, injera, pot-au-feu, ackee and saltfish, ceviche

Answers on p.144 Score

Quiz 74 **Capital Cities**

1. What West African capital is named after a 19th-century US president?

2. Which European capital was renovated and rebuilt by Baron Haussmann in the 1860s, resulting in the creation of several large new boulevards?
A) Berlin, Germany B) Paris, France
C) Brussels, Belgium

3. Founded in 1960, what capital's buildings were mostly designed by Oscar Niemeyer?

4. Kinshasa, the capital of the Democratic Republic of Congo, lies directly across the Congo River from which city, the capital of the Republic of Congo?

5. If the capital cities of all the world's countries were listed alphabetically, which would come first?

6. And which would come last?

7. Marrakesh and Casablanca are probably Morocco's most famous cities, but neither is the capital. What is?

8. Which European capital provided the setting for the 1995 film *Before Sunrise*, starring Ethan Hawke and Julie Delpy?

9. What is the highest capital city in the world?

10. And what is lowest capital city in the world?

11. What European country doesn't officially have a capital according to its constitution? For a bonus point, what city acts as its seat of government?

12. What is the capital of Uzbekistan?

13. Juba is the capital of which recently established country?

14. The name of which European capital translates as 'black pool' in the country's original language?
A) Bucharest, Romania B) Athens, Greece
C) Dublin, Ireland

15. Which European capital city is home to the world's oldest zoo?
A) London B) Paris C) Vienna

16. What Asian capital city is home to the Shinjuku area, famed for its high concentration of skyscrapers?

17. Bamako is the capital of which African country?
A) Mali B) Niger C) Burkina Faso

18. What two cities merged to form a new city in 1873, now the capital of an Eastern European country?

19. What southern hemisphere capital city is this?
A) Canberra, Australia B) Wellington, New Zealand C) Buenos Aires, Argentina

20. The River Danube flows through four capital cities. Can you name them? You get a point for each.

Answers on p.144   Score

Quiz 75 **General Knowledge**

1. When addressing a letter in or to the United States, you need to add a zip code, but what does 'zip' stand for?

2. 90° North is the latitude of what location?

3. Who was the first woman to travel into space? And, for a bonus point, in which year?

4. *Mamajuana* is a herbal liqueur from which Caribbean country?

5. Opened in 1928, the world's first purpose-built international airport was constructed in, and named after, which London suburb?

6. Kutilda Woods, the mother of the US golfer Tiger Woods, was born in which country?

7. Which three countries border Africa's Lake Victoria? You get a point for each.

8. The ruins of the ancient city of Nineveh, once the largest in the world, are located in which modern Middle Eastern country?

9. Native to the deserts of the southwestern United States and northwestern Mexico, what sort of creature is a gila monster?
A) A lizard B) A bird C) A snake

10. What city should you visit if you want to take a look at Leonardo da Vinci's *Last Supper*?

11. In what US state is Mt Rushmore?

12. Luanda is the capital of which African country?

13. The Appia, the Flaminia and the Aemilia are examples of what form of ancient Roman engineering?
A) Bridges B) Roads C) Amphitheatres

14. Located in Jaipur, India, the name of the 18th-century palace the Hawa Mahal translates as what?
A) Pink Palace B) Palace of the Winds
C) Sandstone Palace

15. An oxbow lake is known by what name in Australia?

16. What is the main religion of the people of East Timor?
A) Hinduism B) Islam C) Catholicism

17. What capital city is closest to the Equator?

18. What is this photograph?
A) A close-up of a Roy Lichtenstein pop art painting in MOMA, New York
B) An aerial shot of circular fields in Kansas, USA
C) An ancient map of an Aztec settlement in Mexico

19. Suomi is the native name of which European country?

20. To what countries do these stock market indices belong? You get a point for each.
A) FTSE 100 B) NASDAQ-100 C) CSI 300
D) Nikkei 225 E) CAC 40 F) DAX

© Wikimedia Commons

Quiz 76 **General Knowledge**

1. Highclere Castle in Hampshire, England, was the main setting for which British TV costume drama?

2. What's the oldest game reserve in Africa?
A) Masai Mara National Reserve, Kenya
B) Chobe National Park, Botswana
C) Kruger National Park, South Africa

3. If you were trekking along the Annapurna circuit, where would you be?

4. In what German city could you visit the Mercedes-Benz Museum?

5. What is the name of the large, often dark-coloured clouds that form an anvil-like shape with a flat top, whose presence often means that a thunderstorm is on the way?

6. The Waitomo Caves on New Zealand's North Island are famed for what?
A) Their giant stalactites
B) The glow-worms that illuminate the walls
C) The enormous population of bats

7. In what country would you find the Althing, the world's oldest parliament, founded way back in the year 930?

8. Traditionally, the winner of the Indianapolis 500 motor race celebrates by drinking a bottle of what?

9. What is Europe's only double-landlocked country (surrounded by countries that are also landlocked)?

10. '0 Calm: sea like a mirror', '3 Gentle breeze: large wavelets, perhaps scattered white horselets' and '9 Strong gale: high waves; dense streaks of foam along the direction of the wind; sea begins to roll' are descriptions of the sea's surface using what scale?

11. Albert Einstein started out as a part-time scientist. While formulating his theories of relativity in the early 20th century, his main job was working in a Swiss what?

12. What are the Perseids?
A) A Greek island group
B) A mountain range in Turkmenistan
C) An annual meteor shower

13. Released in 1961, which novel about the Second World War was set on the Italian island of Pianosa?

14. The flag of which African country consists of three horizontal bands of black, red and green, with a red rising sun emerging out of the black band at the top?
A) Madagascar B) Malawi C) Morocco

15. Which ancient Greek mathematician is known as the 'father of geometry' and was the author of the mathematics textbook, *Elements*, still used today?

16. Sargon the Great was the founder of which empire in Mesopotamia in the third millennium BCE, often regarded as the world's first true empire?

17. Which 18th-century adventurer, famed for his colourful love life, was the only person ever to escape from the notorious prison above the Doge's Palace in Venice?

18. What are the 'oysters' in the North American dish, Rocky Mountain oysters? (Clue: they're not oysters.)

19. Found in Africa, what is a turaco?
A) A bird B) A hat C) A cooking pot

20. Can you name the eight European Union countries which don't use the euro as their main currency? You get a point for each.

Answers on p.145   Score

Quiz 77 General Knowledge

1. The Four Corners Monument marks the point where which four US states meet?

2. What was the name of the Roman emperor who in 285 CE divided the empire in two halves: the Western Empire and the Eastern Empire?
A) Nero **B)** Diocletian **C)** Constantine

3. What sort of animal is a quoll?
A) A flightless bird from South America
B) A carnivorous marsupial from Australia
C) A translucent toad from Africa

4. *The Great Wave off Kanagawa* (also known as *The Great Wave*) is a woodblock print by which 19th-century Japanese artist? For a bonus point, what famous Japanese landmark features in the picture?

5. The very first ghetto, from which all others take their name, is in which European city?
A) Venice **B)** Berlin **C)** Vienna

6. Often used in Indian cookery, what sort of vegetable is bhindi?
A) Okra **B)** Aubergine **C)** Pepper

7. Harry Longabaugh was the real name of which Wild West outlaw, made famous in a 1969 film?
A) Billy the Kid **B)** The Sundance Kid
C) Wild Bill Hickok

8. In what year did the Channel Tunnel between England and France open?
A) 1984 **B)** 1990 **C)** 1994

9. What is the name of the giant stone heads carved by the people of the island of Rapa Nui (also known as Easter Island)?

10. Which planet in the solar system has the shortest day?
A) Earth **B)** Mercury **C)** Jupiter

11. The flash freezing process, which kick-started the frozen food industry, was invented by which US naturalist following a trip to Canada in the 1920s? The company he founded still bears his name.

12. Atahualpa was the last ruler of which empire?
A) Maya **B)** Inca **C)** Mauryan (Indian)

13. 1959 saw the unveiling of which new form of sea transport, the brainchild of the British engineer Christopher Cockerell?
A) Jet ski **B)** Hovercraft **C)** Hydrofoil

14. The kwacha is the currency in which African country?
A) Zambia **B)** Tanzania **C)** Rwanda

15. In what country is Abel Tasman National Park located?
A) Australia **B)** New Zealand **C)** Wales

16. Kalaw Lagaw Ya, Warlpiri and Walmajarri are languages spoken in which country?
A) India **B)** Australia **C)** Nigeria

17. The Spanish explorer Juan Ponce de León led the first European expedition to what is now the state of Florida in 1513. According to popular myth, what fantastical object was he searching for there?

18. Located in a volcanic crater, and home to wildebeest, black rhinoceros and a dense population of lions, in what country would you find the Ngorongoro Conservation Area?

19. Angel Falls, the world's highest waterfall, is located in which South American country?

20. Can you name the 13 countries through which the Equator passes? You get a point for each.

Quiz 78 **Food and Drink**

1. Which country produces the largest amount of olive oil?
A) Spain B) Greece C) Italy

2. In the popular South American dish ceviche, how is the fish prepared?
A) Roasted in the oven
B) Flame grilled on a barbecue
C) Cured in a lime juice marinade

3. Originating in Southeast Asia, and probably first cultivated in the Middle East, what spice is, by weight, one of the most expensive foodstuffs in the world?

4. *Xocoatl*, meaning 'bitter water' was an Aztec drink flavoured with what, which proved very popular with Spanish invaders?

5. From 1928 to 1935, the Australian food spread Vegemite changed its name to what?
A) Yeastreat B) Black Malty C) Parwill

6. A French delicacy, what are crépinettes?
A) Small crêpes B) Snails in garlic
C) Small flat sausages

7. Bacon squares, peaches, sugar cookie cubes, a pineapple-and-grapefruit juice drink, and coffee – these are the items that made up the first meal eaten where?

8. The filling of a haggis, Scotland's national dish, is traditionally made using which ground-up parts of a sheep?
A) Legs and loin
B) Brain and kidneys
C) Heart, liver and lungs

9. And what is the filling of a haggis traditionally encased within?

10. Marlborough is the main wine-growing region of which country, accounting for over 75% of its production?

11. A common street-food snack in South Africa, what are 'walkie talkies'?

12. Akane, Crispin and Fuji are all Japanese varieties of which fruit?

13. In what country was chop suey invented?

14. Consumed in Central and South America, what is chicha?
A) A beer made from fermented maize
B) A type of pancake C) A potato stew

15. Originating in Nigeria and eaten widely in West Africa, what is *suya*?

16. In what country was the spicy meat seasoning known as jerk invented?

17. McDonald's is famous for doing its own takes on local cuisines, but which of the following has not been offered on the menu of an international McDonald's?
A) McPinto in Costa Rica
B) McMollette in Mexico
C) McAloo Tikka Burger in India
D) McFish 'n' Chips in England

18. What does the name of the Italian cheese ricotta mean?
A) Rice-like B) Recooked C) Creamy

19. *Calabresa* is a type of sausage from which South American country?

20. What country are the following beer brands originally from (they may now be brewed elsewhere)? You get a point for each.
A) Paulaner B) Tusker C) Chang D) Efes
E) Corona Extra F) Brahma G) Carlsberg
H) Heineken I) Tsingtao J) Victoria Bitter
K) Chimay L) Labatt M) Pilsner Urquell
N) Kingfisher O) Peroni P) Red Stripe
R) Asahi S) Tiger T) Castle Lager, U) Zywiec

Answers on p.146   Score

Quiz 79 **General Knowledge**

1. Claimed to have 832 separate languages, what nation is believed to be the most linguistically diverse place on Earth?

2. A Unesco World Heritage Site famed for its ancient rock-hewn churches, the town of Lalibela is in which African country?
A) Ethiopia B) Mali C) Algeria

3. What is the second largest city in Germany, by population?

4. Phobos and Deimos are the only known moons of which planet in our solar system?

5. Where would you be if you paid a visit to the following places: Melchior, Signy, Casey, Mirny, Syowa and McMurdo?

6. In what South American country would you find this handy-looking sculpture?

7. What is the currency of Uzbekistan?
A) Do'm B) Wo'm C) So'm

8. To which Scandinavian country does the island of Bornholm belong?
A) Denmark B) Sweden C) Norway

9. 'To the red country and part of the gray country of Oklahoma, the last rains came gently, and they did not cut the scarred earth' is the opening line of which 20th-century novel, which documents the effect of a severe drought and dust storms that hit the US and Canadian prairies in the 1930s?

10. In what country would you find Useless Loop Airport?

11. At what French city do the Saône and Rhône rivers merge?
A) Paris B) Lyon C) Toulouse

12. When it achieved independence from the British Empire in 1966, Bechuanaland changed its name to what?

13. Where can you see people climbing towers of buns as part of an annual celebration?

14. Who designed the Iron Bridge, the world's first cast-iron bridge, which was completed in 1779 and still stands in Shropshire, England?
A) Thomas Telford B) Abraham Darby III
C) Isambard Kingdom Brunel

15. The Bata Shoe Museum is located in which city?
A) Las Vegas, USA B) Paris, France
C) Toronto, Canada

16. In what year did Muhammad, the founder of Islam, die?

17. At 300 m (984 ft), the Costanera Center Torre 2 is South America's tallest building. In which country is it located?

18. Kim Jong-un, the current leader of North Korea is the son of the former leader, Kim Jong-il, who was the son of who, the first leader of the country from 1948 to 1994?

19. In 1924, the first Winter Olympic Games were held where?
A) Chamonix B) St Moritz C) Lake Placid

20. What currencies do the following codes represent? You get a point for each.
A) AUD B) BRL C) CNY D) EUR E) GBP
F) INR G) NOK H) RUB I) USD J) ZAR

Quiz 80 **General Knowledge**

1. The world's largest swimming pool is located at the San Alfonso del Mar resort in which South American country?

2. In what European country do people dress in orange to celebrate King's Day in April?

3. Regina is the capital of which Canadian province?
A) Nova Scotia B) Saskatchewan C) Alberta

4. In what Middle Eastern city would you find the Azadi (or Freedom) Tower?
A) Baghdad B) Jerusalem C) Tehran

5. Until it was knocked over by a drunk truck driver in 1973, the Tree of Ténéré was considered the world's most isolated plant. Where was it?
A) Brazil B) Australia C) Niger

6. How did Australia's 17th prime minister, Harold Holt, die in 1967?

7. In what year and in what city was the five-ringed Olympic flag first flown?
A) 1920 in Antwerp B) 1932 in Los Angeles
C) 1968 in Mexico City

8. The Chocolate Hills are a famous tourist attraction in what Southeast Asian country?

9. Other than the sea and sand, what is the main attraction at Maho Beach in the Dutch Caribbean territory of Sint Maarten?
A) Cocktails B) Planes C) Monkeys

10. The Great Blue Hole is a giant sinkhole and popular dive site off the coast of which Central American country?
A) Costa Rica B) Belize C) Panama

11. The Cave of Hands, so-called for the prehistoric paintings of hands adorning its walls, is in which South American country?

12. Consecrated in 805, what is the oldest cathedral in northern Europe, where the Emperor Charlemagne was buried in 814, and where numerous German kings were crowned in the Middle Ages?
A) Cologne Cathedral, Germany
B) St Stephen's Cathedral, Vienna, Austria
C) Aachen Cathedral, Germany

13. How was Ho Chi Minh City in Vietnam known prior to a name change in 1976?

14. Where would you find the world's largest hedge maze?
A) China B) Hawaii, USA C) Germany

15. What animal was introduced to Queensland, Australia, in the 1930s to control pests on Australian sugar plantations, only to become a major pest itself as numbers exploded and the animals began to devour the native wildlife?

16. What European country, with over 187,000 lakes, has been nicknamed 'The Land of Lakes'?

17. In what Asian country is the Kyaiktiyo Pagoda, which is perched precariously on a golden rock?

18. Gozo and Comino are two of the three inhabited islands that make up which country?

19. The Shakespeare play *Measure for Measure* is set in which European city?

20. Six of these countries drive on the left; six drive on the right. All you have to do is say which does which. You get a point for each.
A) Argentina B) Australia C) Brazil
D) Canada E) China F) Japan G) Kenya
H) Pakistan I) Russia J) South Africa
K) UK L) USA

Answers on p.147 Score

Quiz 81 **General Knowledge**

1. What major US airline was founded in 1924 as Huff Daland Dusters, the world's first aerial crop dusting company?
A) American Airlines **B)** Delta Airlines
C) United Airlines

2. Among the most isolated islands on Earth, Heard Island and the McDonald islands belong to which country? And, for a bonus point, what continent are they closest to?

3. The first of what type of temporary accommodation was opened in 1990 in Jukkasjärvi, Sweden?

4. In what year was the travel review website TripAdvisor founded?
A) 1996 **B)** 2000 **C)** 2004

5. *Siafu* is the Swahili word for which type of creature, sometimes used during medical emergencies?

6. There are more than 5000 of what on the rock face of the Cal Orko cliffs in Bolivia?
A) Dinosaur footprints **B)** Condor nests
C) Zip lines

7. In what country is the Pacific Rim National Park located?
A) Japan **B)** Indonesia **C)** Canada

8. *Macropus rufus* is the scientific name of which iconic Australian animal?

9. What Italian soccer player, the world player of the year in 1993, was nicknamed the 'divine ponytail'?

10. Which country banned the wearing of the hat known as the fez in 1925?
A) Saudi Arabia **B)** Turkey **C)** Morocco

11. The new shekel is the currency of which country?

12. Built in 1885 and dubbed the 'world's first skyscraper', how many storeys did Chicago's Home Insurance Building have?
A) 10 **B)** 50 **C)** 100

13. Native to the Democratic Republic of Congo, and unknown to the western world until the 20th century, the elusive jungle-dwelling okapi is most closely related to what other animal?

14. What is the name of the underwater boundary where the North American and Eurasian tectonic plates are splitting apart?

15. Which Scandinavian country has the most northerly capital: Norway, Sweden or Finland? And, for a bonus point, is it further north than Reykjavík, the capital of Iceland?

16. And, by way of contrast, what is the southernmost capital city in the Americas?

17. The Society Islands can be found in what ocean?

18. What non-native bird did the pharmaceutical manufacturer, bird-lover and drama-fan Eugene Schieffelin introduce to New York's Central Park in 1890, supposedly because he wanted America to have every bird mentioned in the plays of William Shakespeare?
A) Starling **B)** Sparrow **C)** Baltimore oriole

19. Puyi, the last emperor of China, was forced to abdicate his title in what year?
A) 1712 **B)** 1812 **C)** 1912

20. Can you name the eight US states and one Canadian province that border the Great Lakes? You get a point for each.

Answers on p.147   Score

Quiz 82 **Museums**

1. It was a legacy in the will of the chemist James Smithson that established the Smithsonian Institution in Washington DC, in 1846. In what country was Smithson born?

2. In what European city would you find The Rubens House, MAS (Museum aan de Stroon) and the Red Star Line Museum?

3. Founded in 1825, the Iziko South African Museum was South Africa's first museum. In what city is it located?

4. Off the coast of which Spanish island would you find the Museo Atlántico, an underwater museum where you can swim with submerged sculptures?
A) Tenerife B) Fuerteventura C) Lanzarote

5. What's the main attraction of the mausoleum of the First Qin Emperor in Xi'an?

6. In which European city would you find the Pergamon Museum?

7. Where is the Scott Polar Research Institute located?
A) Antarctica B) Toronto, Canada
C) Cambridge, England

8. Which country is home to the largest museum in the southern hemisphere?
A) Australia B) South Africa C) Brazil

9. What European capital city is home to the Museum of Broken Relationships?
A) Lisbon, Portugal B) Bucharest, Romania
C) Zagreb, Croatia

10. In what southeast Asian country would you find the Museum of Enduring Beauty?
A) Malaysia B) Indonesia C) Philippines

11. Which monarch founded the State Hermitage Museum in St Petersburg in 1764?

12. In which museum would you find the Rosetta Stone?
A) British Museum, London B) Louvre, Paris
C) Cairo Museum, Egypt

13. In which museum would you find Rembrandt's famous 1642 painting, *The Night Watch*?

14. The Museum of Manufactures and the South Kensington Museum were two early names for which London collection of arts and crafts?

15. In which Argentinian city would you find the Museum of High Altitude Archaeology?
A) Buenos Aires B) Mendoza C) Saltar

16. What sort of exhibits would you find in Paris's Musée Grévin?
A) Cars B) Waxworks C) Weapons

17. What is the name of the world's oldest museum, founded in Oxford in 1677?

18. The Museo Egizio (Egyptian Museum) is located in which Italian city?
A) Florence B) Milan C) Turin

19. In what city would you find the China Science and Technology Museum?
A) Beijing B) Shanghai C) Shenzen

20. What and where is this museum?

Answers on p.148 Score

Quiz 83 **General Knowledge**

1. Which railway station has the most number of platforms in the world? And, for a bonus point, how many platforms does it have?
A) Shinjuku Railway Station, Tokyo
B) Waterloo Station, London
C) Grand Central Terminal, New York

2. The Gorbals is an area in which British city?

3. The Australian dollar was introduced in 1966. What currency did it replace?

4. What gives the Italian cheese *casu marzu* its distinctive taste?
A) White wine B) Truffles C) Live maggots

5. The foot-stamping, spur-jingling, handkerchief-twirling cueca is the national dance of which South American country?

6. Launched in 1958, what was the name of the United States' first satellite?
A) *Explorer 1* B) *Vanguard 1* C) *San Marco 1*

7. The Turquoise Coast is a popular name for a coastal region in which country?
A) Turkey B) Greece C) Cyprus

8. In the German city of Leipzig, there's a museum dedicated to the German baroque composer behind such works as the Brandenburg Concertos and the Goldberg Variations? Who was he?

9. What is the main ingredient of chana masala, a spicy dish popular in Indian and Pakistani cuisine?
A) Lentils B) Chickpeas C) Onions

10. How many rotating capsules are there on the London Eye, the giant Ferris wheel on the south bank of the River Thames, one of London's most popular tourist attractions?
A) 10 B) 32 C) 100

11. Djemaa El Fna is a large square and market place at the centre of which African city?

12. The first edition of the board game Monopoly was based on which city?
A) New York B) Chicago C) Atlantic City

13. France's Musée National d'Arte Moderne is housed in which modernist building, opened in 1977 in Paris?

14. Found in Australia, what sort of creature is a taipan?

15. Which country is sometimes referred to as the Corazón de Sudamérica ('Heart of South America')?

16. In what US city will you find the National Civil Rights Museum? It's round the corner from where Martin Luther King was assassinated in 1968.

17. King Zog I ruled over which European country from 1928 to 1939? What events put a premature end to his reign?

18. Hamilton is the capital of which North Atlantic island, a British Overseas Territory?

19. One of the few places where the critically endangered mountain gorilla can still be found in the wild, Volcanoes National Park is in what African country?

20. What country are the following liqueurs from and what are they flavoured with? You get two points for each. Note, the same country may appear more than once.
A) Bajtra B) Crème de cassis C) Ginja
D) Goldschläger E) Grand Marnier
F) Kahlúa G) Kruškovac H) Limoncello
I) Midori J) Pastis

Quiz 84 **General Knowledge**

1. The flag of which African country has at its centre a red, white and black Masai shield and two crossed spears?

2. What is a quandong?
A) An African bird B) A Chinese fish
C) An Australian fruit

3. An enormous monumental arch known as the 'Gateway to India' was erected in 1911 in which Indian city?

4. In ancient Greece, what was a hoplite?
A) A vase B) A sandal C) A soldier

5. What is the only territory in South America where the euro is the main currency?

6. What animal does this skull belong to?
A) Elephant B) Hippo C) Walrus

7. Which impressionist painter died in 1903 on the island of Atuona in French Polynesia?
A) Paul Gauguin B) Paul Cézanne
C) Pierre Auguste Renoir

8. *Hiten* was a lunar probe launched by which country in 1990?

9. The Doge was the ruler of which European city state from 726 to 1797, when it was overthrown by France?

10. The Australian marsupial, the wombat, produces poop that is shaped like what?
A) Sausages B) Pyramids C) Cubes

11. The bestselling novel *The Kite Runner*, by Khaled Hosseini, is set in which country?

12. Ellen Johnson Sirleaf became Africa's first female head of state when she was elected president of which country in 2006?

13. American, mugger, Orinoco and Nile are all species of what type of animal?

14. Each year in the German town of Bayreuth there is a festival celebrating the music of which composer?

15. What is the name of the military and political leader who in the 19th century helped establish the independence from Spanish rule of what are now Venezuela, Bolivia, Colombia, Ecuador, Peru and Panama?

16. Smørrebrød, an open sandwich using dense rye bread, is a speciality of which Scandinavian country?

17. What was the name of the Benedictine monk who worked in the wine cellar of the Abbaye Saint-Pierre d'Hautvillers, France, in the late 17th century, where he 'invented' champagne?

18. Which African country has the most land borders with other countries?
A) Zambia B) Tanzania
C) Democratic Republic of Congo

19. The volcanic island of Surtsey emerged from beneath the ocean waves in 1963 off the coast of which country?

20. Including the Games of 2020, five cities have hosted the Summer Olympic Games more than once. How many can you name? You get a point for each.

Answers on p.149   Score

Quiz 85 **General Knowledge**

1. Traditionally, when should the German white sausages known as weisswurst be eaten?
A) In the morning B) In the evening
C) At Christmas

2. The flag of which country has a blue 24-spoke wheel, known as the Ashoka Chakra, in its centre?

3. The world's largest church, the Basilica of Our Lady of Peace, is located in which country?
A) USA B) Ivory Coast C) China

4. Which four South American countries have the peso as their currency?

5. The 2001 French film *Amélie* is set in which district of Paris?

6. Related to crickets and weighing up to 70 g (2.5 oz), making them one of the heaviest insects in the world, the giant weta is native to which country?

7. Crop Over is a large carnival-like harvest celebration on which Caribbean island?

8. Found on several Indonesian islands, what sort of animal is a babirusa?

9. Gorée Island, an infamous centre of slave trading in the 18th century, is off the coast of which African country?

10. Which US state was briefly an independent country from 1836 to 1846?

11. What country drinks the most beer per person?
A) Austria B) Czech Republic C) Germany

12. Nassau is the capital of which country of over 700 islands, just north of Cuba?

13. Found across much of the Americas, hummingbirds are the only birds that can hover in mid-air by flapping their wings at great speeds in a figure-of-eight pattern. But just how fast can the fastest flapper flap?
A) 8 beats a second
B) 80 beats a second
C) 800 beats a second

14. All but seven French monarchs were crowned at what cathedral?
A) Reims
B) Notre Dame de Paris
C) Chartres

15. The Temple of the Golden Pavilion is a historic monument and major tourist attraction in which country?
A) China B) Thailand C) Japan

16. Part of Micronesia in the central Pacific, what is the smallest island nation in the world?

17. What African animal's name means 'earth pig' in Afrikaans?

18. In what country is the city of Patras, site of one of Europe's biggest annual carnivals?

19. Name this waterfall.

© Pierpaolo Romano / Shutterstock

20. Can you name the eight countries that have territory inside the Arctic Circle? You get a point for each.

Answers on p.149   Score

Quiz 86 **Seas and Oceans**

1. Roughly what percentage of the Earth's water is in the oceans?
A) 36.5% **B)** 66.5% **C)** 96.5%

2. The Sargasso Sea, an area of the North Atlantic Ocean bounded by four currents, is named after what?

3. What is the name of the gorge in the Mariana Trench that marks the deepest part of the ocean, and the deepest point on the Earth's surface? And, for a bonus point, how deep is it (to within 300 m / 1000 ft)?

4. After the blue whale, what is the second largest animal on Earth?

5. What is the name of the ocean that surrounds Antarctica?

6. The Suez Canal connects which two seas?

7. The Sea of Marmara is an inland sea in which country? And what two bodies of water does it connect?

8. In which appropriately named sea is the Great Barrier Reef located?

9. The three points of Miami, Puerto Rico and Bermuda mark the outer limits of what?

10. Roughly what percentage of the planet's oxygen is produced by marine plants?
A) 30% **B)** 50% **C)** 70%

11. What is the name of the lake between Kazakhstan and Uzbekistan, once one of the four largest in the world, that has shrunk since the 1960s to around 10% of its original size through overuse of its water for irrigation?

12. What is the largest predator in the oceans?

13. Just how big is the Great Pacific Garbage Patch?
A) 160,000 sq km (60,000 sq miles)
B) 1.6 million sq km (600,000 sq miles)
C) 16 million sq km (6 million sq miles)

14. What is the name of the ocean current that originates in the Gulf of Mexico before heading across the Atlantic Ocean to Europe and Africa?

15. What is a seamount?
A) A type of seahorse found in the Atlantic Ocean
B) An undersea volcanic mountain that doesn't reach the water's surface
C) An enormous wave, bigger than an island's highest point

16. What is the name of the process by which certain creatures, including some species of anglerfish and plankton, are able to produce their own light?

17. There are three main categories of sea life: plankton, nekton and benthos. What is the difference between them?

18. Name the oil rig that exploded and sank in 2010 in the Gulf of Mexico causing the biggest oil spill in US history.

19. Inhabiting kelp forests along the edges of the Pacific Ocean, what marine mammal has the densest fur of any animal?

20. What name is given to the large flat areas of the sea floor between 3000 m (9800 ft) and 6000 m (20,000 ft)?
A) Hadal Zone
B) Abyssal Plain
C) Oceanic Trenches

Answers on p.150   Score

Quiz 87 **General Knowledge**

1. Roughly how many people live in Greenland, the world's most sparsely populated territory?
A) 5500 **B)** 55,00 **C)** 555,000

2. Descending to 1642 m (5387 ft), what is the deepest lake on Earth?

3. In what year did Athens play host to the first Olympic Games of modern times?

4. Found in eastern and southern Africa, what sort of animal is a klipspringer?
A) A giant grasshopper
B) A medium-sized bird
C) A small antelope

5. If you're strolling through Bogotá tucking into a *bollo*, where are you and what are you eating?

6. In geographical terms, what is the opposite of oriental?

7. What political leader said the following at his 1922 trial for sedition: 'Non-violence is the first article of my faith. It is also the last article of my creed'?

8. In what Canadian city did the film stars Elizabeth Taylor and Richard Burton get married in 1964? And, for a bonus point, in which African country is the village of Kasane where they got married for a second time?

9. The port of Fray Bentos, once home to a major meat-processing industry (and after which the famous processed meat company is named), is in which South American country?

10. Who is the award-winning Australian writer whose works include *Oscar and Lucinda* and the *True History of the Kelly Gang*?

11. In what European country would you find the ski resort of Courmayeur?
A) Italy **B)** France **C)** Switzerland

12. What country was known from 1955 to 1971 as East Pakistan?

13. What is the currency of Egypt?
A) Egyptian pound **B)** Egyptian dollar
C) Egyptian franc

14. What European nation has two heads of state, neither of which reside in the country?

15. The lost colony of Roanoke, England's first failed attempt to establish a permanent settlement in North America, was in which modern US state?

16. Who succeeded Joseph Stalin as leader of the Soviet Union in 1953?

17. The giant anteater is native to which continent?

18. *Tā moko* is the traditional Māori practice of what?
A) Wood carving **B)** Tattooing
C) Canoe building

19. What city is this?
A) Pyongyang **B)** Moscow **C)** Beijing

© artistVMG / Shutterstock

20. Can you name the seven countries that make up Central America, not including Mexico? You get a point for each.

Quiz 88 **General Knowledge**

1. The *stroopwafel*, a thin chequered waffle with a caramel syrup filling, is a favourite treat from which country?
A) Belgium B) Italy C) The Netherlands

2. What river forms around 850 km (530 miles) of the border between Thailand and Laos?

3. What is the third brightest object in the sky, after the Sun and Moon?

4. London Zoo is located in which of the city's royal parks?

5. The term porteño, meaning 'port person', is often used to describe the inhabitants of which South American capital city?

6. Rottnest Island, a small island just off the coast of Perth/Fremantle is home to most of the world's population of which marsupial?

7. Which European capital city boasts a giant stone monument on its seafront called the Monument of the Discoveries, celebrating the country's seafaring and exploring past?
A) Rome B) Athens C) Lisbon

8. The invention of the Caesar salad is generally attributed to the Italian chef Caesar Cardini, who came up with the recipe in 1924 at his restaurant in which country?
A) Italy B) USA C) Mexico

9. The 1864–66 Chincha Islands War between Spain and its former colonies, Chile and Peru, was fought over the control of which product, then abundant on the islands?

10. Cabo Verde is the most westerly country on which continent?

11. What is the only country to have a five-sided flag?

12. *Kifto* is a dish of spiced raw beef eaten on special occasions in which African country?
A) Tunisia B) Ethiopia C) Namibia

13. Discovered in 1869 in Moliagul, Victoria, Australia, the Welcome Stranger is the largest example of a what ever found?
A) Alluvial gold nugget
B) Gem-quality rough diamond
C) Quartz crystal cluster

14. In the 19th century, a pair of ancient obelisks were exported from Egypt and erected in London and New York. By what name are both these obelisks known today?

15. Now a national monument open for public tours, Fort Sumter was where the first shots of the American Civil War were fired in 1861. It lies off the coast of which state?
A) Florida B) North Carolina
C) South Carolina

16. In Homer's *Odyssey*, Odysseus spends ten years trying to return to which Greek island after the Trojan War?
A) Crete B) Santorini C) Ithaca

17. Utah, Omaha, Gold, Juno and Sword were the code names for what?

18. Famed for their intricately crafted gold ornaments, the culture of the Zenú people lasted from around 200 BCE to 1600 CE in which South American country?

19. Designed by Britain's Isambard Kingdom Brunel, what was the world's largest ship from 1858 to 1899?
A) SS *Great Eastern* B) SS *Great Western*
C) SS *Great Northern*

20. Canada is made up of 10 provinces and three territories. How many can you name? You get a point for each.

Answers on p.150 Score

Quiz 89 **General Knowledge**

1. Pecorino is an Italian cheese made from the milk of which animal?
A) Cow B) Sheep C) Goat

2. The Gangotri Glacier is one of the main sources of which major Asian river?

3. The South African city of Kimberley is named after a nearby kimberlite pipe. What would you find in a kimberlite pipe?

4. Which Pacific country is the first in the world to welcome the new year?
A) Kiribati B) Samoa C) Tonga

5. *Tejo*, a popular sport in Colombia, involves throwing a small metal disc at a target packed with what?
A) Sweets B) Gunpowder C) Flowers

6. What is the name of the Tudor warship of Henry VIII that sank during a battle with the French in 1545 off the south coast of England, but was then raised from the seabed in 1982?

7. Reaching a depth of 12,262 m (40,230 ft), the deepest human-made hole ever dug, the Kola Superdeep Borehole, is in what country?

8. Halifax is the capital of which Canadian province?

9. What is wider, Australia or the contiguous United States of America?

10. What is the only one of New York's five boroughs located on the US mainland?

11. Eris, Makemake and Haumea are all types of what?
A) Volcano B) Pacific island C) Dwarf planet

12. Singha is a brand of beer from which Asian country?

13. Ucayali, Marañón, Negro and Xingu are all tributaries of which major river?

14. All pet hamsters are related to a single breeding pair captured in the 1930s in which country?
A) Turkey
B) Syria
C) Egypt

15. According to the International Union for the Conservation of Nature, what is the most trafficked animal in the world, accounting for around 20% of the illegal wildlife trade?
A) Pangolin
B) Grey Parrot
C) Squirrel monkey

16. Italy shares its northern border with which four countries? You need to get all four for a point.

17. One of the world's most easily accessible volcanoes, where people can often go right up to the crater's edge to watch lava erupting, Mt Yasur is located on which island nation?
A) Vanuatu B) Stromboli C) Iceland

18. The city of Carthage, which in ancient times controlled a vast Mediterranean empire before being defeated and swallowed up by Rome in the second century BCE, was in which modern country?

19. In what year did the US city of St Louis host the Summer Olympic Games?
A) 1904 B) 1924 C) 1954

20. The Danube passes through or alongside 10 countries, more than any other river. How many can you name? You get a point for each. And, for a bonus point, into what body of water does it empty?

Answers on p.151   Score

Quiz 90 **Space**

1. What became the first human-made object to go into space on 3 October 1942?
A) A Japanese weather balloon
B) A German V2 rocket
C) A British spitfire with broken controls

2. Other than our Sun, what's the closest star to Earth? And, assuming you could travel at the speed of light, how long would it take you to get there?

3. Launched in 1959, the Soviet spacecraft *Luna 3* took the first ever close-up photographs of what?

4. ISRO is the space agency of which country?

5. What was the first space station called?
A) Salyut 1 B) Skylab C) Soyuz II

6. What is Baikonur?
A) A comet that visits the inner solar system every 62 years
B) The site of Russia's main space launch facility
C) A space probe that flew past Venus in the early 1970s

7. In July 2015, *New Horizons* became the first spacecraft to make a fly-by past what major body in the solar system?

8. Roughly how much of the solar system's mass is contained in the Sun?
A) 50% B) 75% C) 99.8%

9. What was the first rover to explore the Martian surface?
A) *Sojourner* B) *Opportunity* C) *Curiosity*

10. How fast does sound travel in space?
A) Faster than on Earth
B) Slower than on Earth
C) It doesn't travel at all

11. In 1984, the American astronaut Bruce McCandless performed the first untethered spacewalk using a jetpack called an MMU. What does MMU stand for?

12. In what year did a space shuttle first make it into space? And, for a bonus point, what was the name of the shuttle?

13. In 1949, the British astronomer Fred Hoyle coined which term to describe the then new theory of the origin of the universe?

14. Launched in 1995 and still operating today, SOHO is a spacecraft designed to study which body in the solar system?

15. Between 2011 and 2015, the spacecraft *Dawn* visited the protoplanets Vesta and Ceres. Where in the solar system are these bodies located?

16. In what year did Yang Liwei become the first person to be sent into space by China's space programme?
A) 1983 B) 1993 C) 2003

17. So far, what is the only spacecraft to have visited Uranus and Neptune?
A) *Pioneer 10* B) *Voyager 2* C) *Juno*

18. What was the name of the first American woman in space? And, for a bonus point, in what year did she achieve this feat?

19. What spacecraft is the most expensive machine ever constructed?

20. What planets (or dwarf planets) do the following moons orbit? You get two points for each.
A) Charon B) Triton C) Titania
D) Enceladus E) Callisto

Answers on p.151 Score

Quiz 91 **General Knowledge**

1. The Hollywood sign that overlooks Los Angeles used to say what?

2. Often claimed to be the widest avenue in the world with a mighty 16 lanes of traffic, in what South American city would you find Avenida 9 de Julio?

3. According to tradition, the Viking Ingólfur Arnarson founded which European capital city in the year 874?

4. An armed rebellion by gold miners in the Australian mining town of Ballarat in 1851, which led to the British government granting voting rights to all male colonists, is known by what name?

5. Which city was originally supposed to host the 1908 Olympics, but withdrew when a nearby volcano erupted, thereby handing the games to London?
A) Jakarta, Indonesia B) Mexico City, Mexico C) Rome, Italy

6. What North African city is nicknamed the 'Red City'?

7. Which US architect designed the Guggenheim Museum in Bilbao?

8. Opened in 1986, the Lotus Temple is a Baha'i house of worship shaped like a lotus flower in which Indian city?

9. What is the name of the royal residence on the Isle of Wight where Queen Victoria died in 1901?

10. With average rainfall of less than 1 mm (0.04 in) a year, what is the driest desert on Earth?

11. Which early US president designed his own house, named Monticello, on his plantation in Virginia?

12. In a country famed for its runners, the Great Ethiopian Run is an annual 10-km event held in which city?

13. In the 19th century, Lake Wenham in Massachusetts was a major source of what commodity, widely sold in the UK?

14. A picturesque 300 km (190 mile) stretch of which country's coast is known as the Garden Route?

15. The world's oldest international sporting trophy, first competed for in 1851, the America's Cup is held in which sport?

16. *Cichetti* are small tapas-like snacks served in the bars of which Italian city?

17. Opened in 1583, Dyrehavsbakken, the world's oldest continually operating theme park, is in what country?

18. The Pan-American Highway is a network of roads stretching for 30,000 km (19,000 miles) from the top of Canada to the foot of South America, apart from a small 106 km (66 mile) break owing to thick impenetrable jungle on the border of which two countries?

19. Museumsinsel ('Museum Island'), the site of several major collections, is located on a river in which German city?

20. Can you match the cheese to the country? You get a point for each.
Cheeses: **A)** Emmental **B)** Cotija
C) Marscapone **D)** Gouda **E)** Feta
F) Domiati **G)** Manchego **H)** Halloumi
I) Stilton **J)** Paneer **K)** Roquefort **L)** Adelost

Countries: Sweden, France, India, England, Cyprus, Spain, Egypt, Greece, Netherlands, Italy, Mexico, Switzerland

Quiz 92 **General Knowledge**

1. You're eating a hot dog bought from a *pølsevogn* and washing it down with a chocolate milk – where are you?

2. Believed to exist (though never directly observed) in the outer solar system, the Oort Cloud is made up mainly of what?

3. From what language does the word 'safari' derive?

4. In what US state is the town of Punxsutawney where the main Groundhog Day celebrations are held every 2 February?

5. In what US state is the town of Punxsutawney where the main Ground Hog Day celebrations are held every 2 February?

6. Located in Portugal, what is Cabo da Roca's claim to fame?
A) It was voted the country's most idyllic spot in an online poll
B) It is mainland Europe's westernmost spot
C) It's the location of the Portuguese prime minister's official holiday retreat

7. In what Australian city were the 1956 Summer Olympic Games held?

8. Currently the home of the prime minister, and formerly the residence of the emperor, the Menelik Palace (also known as the Gebi) is in which African country?
A) Morocco **B)** Senegal **C)** Ethiopia

9. The oil tanker *Exxon Valdez* caused a major oil spill and environmental disaster in 1989 when it ran aground off the coast of which US state?

10. Also known as the 'Shuk', the Mahane Yehuda Market is a large marketplace in which Middle Eastern city?

11. What's the UK's longest river?

12. Yellowknife is the capital of which Canadian Territory?

13. What is the name of the Indian city on the Ganges, a major site of pilgrimage for many Hindus who perform ritual ablutions on stone embankments known as ghats?

14. Thought to have more boats per person than any other city on Earth, what southern hemisphere city is nicknamed the 'City of Sails'?

15. What was the name of the spacecraft launched by the European Space Agency in 2004 which, in 2014, became the first spacecraft to orbit a comet?

16. Bunny chow, consisting of a quarter loaf of bread filled with curry, is a popular street food in which African country?

17. What is generally regarded as the southernmost city in the world?
A) Ushuaia, Argentina
B) Cape Town, South Africa
C) Invercargill, New Zealand

18. In Barcelona, people celebrate the annual festival of La Mercè with food, fireworks, parades and activities, including building *castellers*. What is a *casteller*?

19. A golden spike was symbolically driven into the rails to mark the completion of what in 1869?

20. Can you name the 15 current (as of June 2018) members of OPEC (the Organisation of the Petroleum Exporting Countries)? You get a point for each.

Answers on p.152   Score ☐

Quiz 93 **General Knowledge**

1. In what year was the US city of Las Vegas founded?
A) 1805 B) 1855 C) 1905

2. Found in the Amazon and Orinoco rivers, what sort of animal is a boto?

3. What's the difference between a hurricane, a typhoon and a cyclone?
A) Wind speed
B) Amount of rain released C) Nothing

4. A traditional harvest ritual on Pentecost Island in Vanuatu was the inspiration behind which modern extreme sport?
A) Kitesurfing B) Wingsuit flying
C) Bungee jumping

5. In 1820, the Russian naval officer Fabian Gottlieb von Bellingshausen became the first person to set eyes on what part of the world?

6. The European Central Bank has its headquarters in which city?
A) London B) Frankfurt C) Brussels

7. What is the name of the United States central bank and where is it based?

8. And what is the name of China's central bank and where is it based?

9. Formerly a colony controlled by the Netherlands, the Dutch East Indies achieved independence in 1949 as what country?

10. The 1947 play (and later film) *A Streetcar Named Desire* by Tennessee Williams is set in which US city?

11. A Vietnamese snack, what sort of food is a banh mi?

12. On what Mediterranean island would you find Cape Carbonara?

13. Which European country is home to the world's largest permanent scale model of the solar system?
A) England B) Sweden C) Bulgaria

14. Inhabiting tropical islands across the Indian and Pacific oceans, what is the world's largest land-living invertebrate?

15. Castillo de San Felipe de Barajas, Spain's largest overseas fortress during the days of empire, stands in which South American city, once a major target for pirates?

16. The Dancing House (also known as 'Fred and Ginger'), so-called because it resembles a gyrating couple, is a modernist building in which European capital?

17. Goat Island divides what natural wonder on the border of Canada and the USA?

18. From 1930 to 1970, the Jules Rimet Trophy was awarded to the winners of what? And, for a bonus point, why was it no longer awarded after this date?

19. This is the ceiling of which famous Italian building?
A) Milan Cathedral B) The Pantheon, Rome
C) Florence Cathedral

© Pavel Ilyukhin / Shutterstock

20. Can you name the 12 countries who have hosted the Winter Olympics (including one now defunct nation)? You get a point for each.

Answers on p.153   Score

Quiz 94 **Changing Places**

Here are a few testing questions on places that have
changed their names or locations.

1. Prior to German reunification in the 1990s, what was the capital of West Germany?

2. Which two areas (one mainland, one an archipelago) joined together to form the new country of Tanzania in 1964?

3. In 1950, the small New Mexico town of Hot Springs changed its name to what, in order to feature on a then popular radio game show?

4. In the 1960s, which city was built to replace Karachi as the capital of Pakistan? And, while it was being built, which city served as the interim capital from 1958 to 1967?

5. It's now known as the Democratic Republic of Congo, as it was between 1965 and 1971, but what was this country called from 1971 to 1997?

6. This is the parliament house of which purpose-built capital, which replaced its predecessor in 1927?

7. In 1925, this Scandinavian capital changed its name from Kristiania to what?

8. When Turkey was established in 1923, following the fall of the Ottoman Empire, its capital was sited, not in the old imperial capital of Istanbul, but where?

9. Brazil's capital is now Brasília. But what was it up until 1961?

10. The new country of Zimbabwe emerged out of a civil war in 1980 from which former British colony?

11. India's capital moved from Calcutta (now Kolkata) to what in 1911?

12. Tokyo became Japan's capital city in 1868 when the Emperor Meiji moved his seat from what other city? (Clue: it's an anagram of the new city.)

13. Russia's capital was moved from which city to Moscow in 1918?

14. Made up of 115 islands, which country in the Indian Ocean was originally known as the 'Seven Sisters'?

15. In 1935, Persia officially changed its name to what?

16. What country was known as the Khmer Republic from 1970 to 1975 and Democratic Kampuchea from 1975 to 1979?

17. What country was formerly known as The Gold Coast?

18. In 1932, Siam officially changed its name to what?

19. The central American country of Belize was once which British colony?

20. Batavia is the former name of which Southeast Asian capital city?

Answers on p.153   Score [ ]

Quiz 95 **General Knowledge**

1. The Navajo Nation, the largest single Native American territory, occupies portions of Arizona, Utah and what other US state?

2. What do Penhill in England, Brynhill in Wales and Bergeberbet in Norway have in common, linguistically speaking?

3. Krungthepmahanakhon Amonrattanakosin Mahintharayutthaya Mahadilokphop Noppharatratchathaniburirom Udomratchaniwetmahasathan Amonphimanawatansathit Sakkathattiyawitsanukamprasit is the full ceremonial name of which Asian capital city?

4. The Bruce Highway runs for around 1600 km (1000 miles) along the east coast of which country?
A) Canada B) Australia C) South Africa

5. In 1984, the West African country of Upper Volta changed its name to what?

6. What was name of the first chimpanzee sent into space in 1961?
A) Ham B) Eggs C) Bacon

7. Cantopop is a genre of popular music from which Asian city?
A) Hong Kong B) Singapore C) Japan

8. Frederick Law Olmstead is famed for designing which major New York attraction?
A) Empire State Building B) Carnegie Hall
C) Central Park

9. Jonestown, the settlement established under the cult leadership of the Reverend Jim Jones, and the site of a mass suicide in 1978, was in which country?

10. In which African country would you find the city of Chefchaouen, best known for its buildings painted in various shades of blue?

11. Harry Beck is famed as the man behind which iconic London design?
A) The red telephone box B) The black taxi
C) The Tube map

12. What is Lake Compounce's claim to fame?
A) It's Mexico's longest lake
B) It's Canada's largest artificial lake
C) It's the USA's oldest amusement park

13. The largest-known cave chamber in the world (by area) is in which country?
A) Malaysia B) USA C) Tanzania

14. In what year did the Western Roman Empire come to an end when the last Roman emperor, Romulus Augustulus, abdicated?
A) 410 B) 476 C) 1453

15. Believed by many scholars to be the world's oldest cathedral, the Etchmiadzin Cathedral is in what country?
A) Armenia B) Georgia C) Lebanon

16. On which country's coast would you find the Bay of Plenty?

17. What sort of tree is the famous Gran Gomero, a great sprawling 50-m (164-ft) giant in the Recoleta district of Buenos Aires, which was planted more than 200 years ago?

18. The Olduvai Gorge, where the remains of many early human species, including *Homo habilis* and *Homo erectus*, have been found, is in which African country?

19. By what name is Saloth Sar, the infamous former leader of the Khmer Rouge, better known?

20. The Rhine River begins in Switzerland, flowing through Liechtenstein, Austria, Germany and France, before entering which country where it meets the sea?

Quiz 96 **General Knowledge**

1. In what US city would you find the Atomic Testing Museum, the Neon Museum and the Burlesque Hall of Fame?

2. What African country has the world's largest population of cheetahs?
A) Kenya B) Zimbabwe C) Namibia

3. Listed by Unesco as a 'Masterpiece of the Oral and Intangible Heritage of Humanity', the Carnaval de Oruro takes place in which South American country?

4. In which country is the hongi performed, a traditional greeting where people press their noses together?

5. Bloomsday, held on 16 June in Dublin, Ireland, is a celebration of which novel?

6. St George is the capital of which Caribbean island, which was briefly invaded by the US in 1983?

7. Built in 1642, Copenhagen's Rundetårn (Round Tower) is Europe's oldest what?
A) Observatory B) Brewery C) Restaurant

8. Popular in Argentina, the game of *pato* is now played using a leather ball, but what did players originally use?
A) A large coconut B) A live duck
C) A dead fish

9. The traditional El Colacho Festival in Castillo de Murcia, Spain, sees men dressed as the devil jumping over what?
A) Bonfires B) Streams C) Babies

10. The Blue Penny Museum, dedicated to the art and history of Mauritius, is located in the country's capital. What is a 'blue penny'?

11. What is China's most common surname?
A) Li B) Chen C) Wang

12. What is this sculpture of two giant horses' heads in the Scottish town of Falkirk called?

13. Bibimbap is a traditional rice dish from which national cuisine?

14. Greater, lesser, Chilean, James's, Andean and American are the six recognised species of which bird?

15. The British merchant navy officer Edward Smith is best known for what?

16. Where on Earth would you find the Mohorovičić discontinuity?
A) Above your head – marking the boundary between Earth and space
B) Below your feet, marking the boundary between the Earth's crust and mantle
C) In ancient Egypt, marking the time between two dynasties

17. Chipolopolo (meaning 'The Copper Bullets') is the nickname of which African country's football team?

18. Palma is the capital and airport of which Spanish island?

19. Sometimes known as the Christmas Witch, La Befana is an old woman said to deliver presents to children on the eve of Epiphany in which European country?

20. What does Unesco stand for?

Answers on p.154   Score ☐

Quiz 97 **US State Capitals**

Can you choose the correct state capital from the three options available? It's tricky – it's not always the one you think it is.

1. Alabama
A) Birmingham
B) Montgomery
C) Mobile

2. Alaska
A) Anchorage
B) Juneau
C) Kodiak

3. California
A) San Francisco
B) Los Angeles
C) Sacramento

4. Colorado (the capital is pictured below)
A) Boulder
B) Denver
C) Colorado Springs

5. Connecticut
A) Bridgeport
B) Stamford
C) Hartford

6. Florida
A) Miami
B) Tallahassee
C) Orlando

7. Georgia
A) Atlanta
B) Augusta
C) Tbilisi

8. Illinois
A) Chicago
B) Springfield
C) Joliet

9. Iowa
A) Sioux City
B) Des Moines
C) Cedar Rapids

10. Kansas
A) Topeka
B) Wichita
C) Kansas City

11. Kentucky
A) Frankfort
B) Louisville
C) Lexington

12. Louisiana
A) Baton Rouge
B) New Orleans
C) Lafayette

13. Massachusetts
A) Boston
B) Plymouth
C) Salem

14. Nevada
A) Reno
B) Carson City
C) Las Vegas

15. Michigan
A) Detroit
B) Grand Rapids
C) Lansing

16. Minnesota (the capital is pictured below)
A) St Paul
B) Minneapolis
C) Duluth

17. New Mexico
A) Albuquerque
B) Santa Fe
C) Roswell

18. New York
A) New York City
B) Buffalo
C) Albany

19. North Carolina
A) Raleigh
B) Charlotte
C) Greensboro

20. Ohio
A) Columbus
B) Cincinnati
C) Cleveland

21. Oregon
A) Salem
B) Portland
C) Eugene

22. Pennsylvania
A) Pittsburgh
B) Harrisburg
C) Philadelphia

23. Texas
A) Austin
B) Houston
C) Dallas

24. Utah (the capital is pictured below)
A) Moab
B) St George
C) Salt Lake City

25. Washington
A) Seattle
B) Olympia
C) Tacoma

Answers on p.154   Score

Quiz 98 **General Knowledge**

1. What group of Pacific islands did the British explorer Captain Cook name the Sandwich Islands in 1778 (shortly before he was killed there)?

2. What cheese is used at the annual Cooper's Hill Cheese-Rolling competition in Gloucestershire, England?
A) Cheddar B) Edam C) Double Gloucester

3. The Gate of the Sun is a giant megalithic stone arch constructed by the Tiwanaku culture of which South American country?

4. What is the most common wild bird in the world?
A) Rock dove (or common pigeon)
B) House sparrow C) Red-billed quelea

5. In what country would you find Namadgi National Park?
A) Australia B) Papua New Guinea
C) New Zealand

6. Y Wladfa is a small settlement in Argentina established in 1865 by settlers from which European country?

7. In what French city did Germany officially surrender to the Allied Powers on 7 May 1945?
A) Paris B) Calais C) Reims

8. What is the name of the currency shared by eight West African countries: Benin, Burkina Faso, Guinea-Bissau, Ivory Coast, Mali, Niger, Senegal and Togo?

9. *Il Milione* is the Italian title of a 13th-century book about which explorer's travels through Asia?

10. Vishnu ('the preserver') and Shiva ('the destroyer') are two of the Gods in the Hindu triumvirate (or '*trimurti*'). Who's the third?

11. What African lake is known as 'Calendar Lake' because it's roughly 365 miles long and 52 miles wide?

12. Me'orav Yerushalmi is a breakfast dish made of various grilled meats that's a speciality of which city?

13. In what Brazilian city would you find the Amazonas Opera House?

14. Believed by many to be England's oldest pub, Ye Olde Trip to Jerusalem is in which city?
A) Leeds B) London C) Nottingham

15. What flower is most associated with Mexico's Day of the Dead Festival?
A) Rose B) Lily C) Marigold

16. Mt Ossa is the highest mountain on which southern island?
A) Sri Lanka B) Tasmania C) South Georgia

17. In what country would you find La Capilla del Hombre, a museum dedicated to the peoples of Latin America?

18. In the German town of Wittenberg, you can visit the Castle Church where the religious reformer Martin Luther nailed his objections or 'theses' against the Catholic church to the door, kick-starting Europe's Protestant Reformation. How many theses did he write?
A) 12 B) 95 C) 666

19. The Gateway Arch, which at 192 m (630 ft) is the world's tallest human-made arch, is in which US city?

20. Can you name the eight countries through which the prime meridian, the line of 0° longitude, passes through? There are three in Europe and five in Africa. You get a point for each.

Answers on p.155 Score

Quiz 99 **General Knowledge**

1. At 5068 years old, the oldest-known living individual tree is located in the White Mountains of California. What species is it?
A) Bristlecone pine B) Patagonian cypress C) Giant Redwood

2. What was the first capital of Italy after it became a united kingdom in 1861? And for a bonus point, what city succeeded it as capital from 1865 to 1870, before Rome finally took over?

3. What is the name of the critically endangered antelope with a large trunk-like nose, which can now be found only in small parts of Russia and Kazakhstan?
A) Eland B) Nyala C) Saiga

4. During the 14th century, seven popes resided in which French city rather than in Rome?

5. In what Asian country is Nguyen by far the most popular surname, shared by around 40% of the population?

6. Morna is a style of music and dance from which African country?
A) Nigeria B) Cabo Verde C) Morocco

7. In 2005, the NASA space probe *Huygens* landed on the largest moon of which planet?

8. What is the capital of the Australian state of Queensland?

9. What percentage of the Earth's atmosphere is carbon dioxide?
A) 40% B) 4% C) 0.04%

10. The Lion and Unicorn Pavilion, the Sea and Ships Pavilion, and a giant cigar-shaped structure called the Skylon were all built in London in 1951 for which celebration?

11. Opened in 1893, and now a National Historic Site of Canada, in what city is the grand castle-like hotel, Château Frontenac?

12. In what Chinese city would you find the China Art Museum, housed in a pavilion built for Expo 2010?
A) Hong Kong B) Shanghai C) Beijing

13. In what city would you find this arch?

14. Who was the first person to break the sound barrier in level flight?

15. Found in South and Central America, what sort of animal is a great curassow?
A) A reptile B) A fish C) A bird

16. What African country has flag showing a cross formed by an AK-47 and a hoe?

17. The Sinulog-Santo Niño Festival is an annual cultural and religious event held in which country?

18. In 1868, the Japanese city of Edo changed its name to what?

19. The country of Cameroon is named after what animal?
A) Elephant B) Lion C) Shrimp

20. Can you name the seven countries that emerged from Yugoslavia after the country broke up in the 1990s? You get a point for each.

Answers on p.155 Score

Quiz 100 **General Knowledge**

Let's finish with a few particularly fiendish teasers.
You might want to think about each one a little bit before giving your answer.

1. Kingstown is the capital city of which Caribbean nation?

2. The Canary Islands are named after which type of animal?

3. What was the name of the defensive wall built in c. 142 CE in Scotland that marked the northern limit of Roman control in Britain?

4. What was the first name of the Indian political activist Gandhi?

5. From what prison was Nelson Mandela released in 1990?

6. In what city would you find Strawberry Fields?

7. If travelling overland from Finland to North Korea, what's the smallest number of countries you would have to pass through?
A) 1
B) 7
C) 15

8. Globally, what was the biggest cause of death among young men in the 1910s?

9. What African country has the greatest number of pyramids?

10. If you were sailing through the Panama Canal from the Pacific Ocean to the Atlantic Ocean, in what direction would you be heading, roughly speaking?

11. Danny Boyle's adaptation of Irvine Welsh's novel *Trainspotting* was mainly filmed in which city?

12. In addition to all the animals, how many people were there on Noah's Ark?

13. How long did the Hundred Years War Last?
A) 99 years
B) 100 years
C) 116 years

14. In what country are Bugatti cars made?
A) Italy B) France C) Argentina

15. What mountain (pictured here) lies furthest from the Earth's core?
A) Everest, Nepal/China
B) Mauna Kea, Hawaii, USA
C) Chimborazo, Ecuador

16. In what month did Russia's October Revolution take place?

17. What company is the world's leading producer of tyres?

18. What colour is the 'black box' flight recorder carried by planes?

19. Who became President of Germany in 1932? Clue: his surname begins with 'H'.

20. As of March 2019, how many stars are there on the flag of the European Union?

Chapter 3

Answers

Answers

Quiz 71
Lonely Planet
1. Lima, Peru
2. Okavango Delta, Botswana
3. Nepal
4. Easter Island
5. Las Vegas, USA
6. York, UK
7. Paris, France
8. Lagos, Nigeria
9. Antarctica
10. New Zealand
11. Everglades, Florida, USA
12. Tokyo, Japan

Quiz 72
1. C) Cleveland, Ohio, USA
2. C) South Africa
3. B) Saudi Arabia. King Fahd's Fountain in Jeddah shoots water taken from the Red Sea up to a height of 260 m (853 ft).
4. B) Washington DC
5. C) Italy
6. B) Denmark
7. C) South Korea
8. Ernest Rutherford
9. Argentina
10. Mt Everest
11. A) Addis Ababa, Ethiopia
12. C) Estonia
13. C) Jericho, Palestinian Territories
14. Galápagos Islands and the Seychelles
15. 1960, from France
16. C) Afghanistan
17. A) Thomas
18. Ecuador
19. C) Australia. It lies to the east of the mainland.
20. Afghanistan, Kazakhstan, Kyrgyzstan, Tajikistan and Turkmenistan

Quiz 73
1. Hindi and English. There are 22 official languages in India.
2. Argentina
3. The Treaty of Versailles
4. B) A wind
5. Sirius, also known as the Dog Star or Alpha Canis Majoris.
6. Mt Tambora. It threw so much dust up into the atmosphere that harvests were devastated across the world and 1816 became known as the 'year without summer'.
7. The Eiger
8. New Zealand
9. Namibia
10. B) 1947
11. Venezuela
12. Boris Becker. He was also the youngest (at 17) and the first unseeded player to do so.
13. Stalingrad
14. No. 10 Downing Street
15. Opal
16. Japan's Emperor Hirohito (under pressure from the United States following his country's defeat in the Second World War)
17. Blackbeard the pirate
18. Brazil
19. Morocco. The goats climb the argan trees to eat its fruit, encouraged by local farmers. The goats cannot digest the nut at the heart of the fruit, which is passed out in their droppings. These can then be collected and used to extract argan oil.
20. A) Austria = Wiener schnitzel, B) Albania = tavë kosi, C) Barbados = cou-cou and flying fish, D) Canada = poutine, E) Ethiopia = injera, F) Finland = karjalanpaisti,
G) France = pot-au-feu,
H) Georgia = khachapuri,
I) Jamaica = ackee and saltfish,
J) Lebanon = kibbeh,
K) Peru = ceviche, L) South Korea = kimchi

Quiz 74
Capital Cities
1. Monrovia, the capital of Liberia, which was named in honour of James Monroe, the fifth US president.
2. B) Paris, France
3. Brasília
4. Brazzaville
5. Abu Dhabi, United Arab Emirates
6. Zagreb, Croatia
7. Rabat
8. Vienna
9. There are two possible answers for this. La Paz, Bolivia at 3,650 m (11,975 ft) above sea level is the answer usually given. However, La Paz is just Bolivia's seat of government, not its constitutional capital; that's Sucre. So, if La Paz is disqualified, then the title goes to the next highest, also in South America: Quito, Ecuador at 2850 m (8612 ft).
10. There's just one answer here: Baku, Azerbaijan which has an average elevation of 28 m (92 ft) below sea level.
11. Switzerland. Bern.
12. Tashkent
13. South Sudan
14. C) Dublin, from the Gaelic 'dubh linn'.
15. C) Vienna, where the Tiergarten Scönbrunn was founded as a royal menagerie in 1752.

Answers

16. Tokyo

17. A) Mali

18. Buda and Pest, which combined to form Budapest, the capital of Hungary.

19. B) Wellington, New Zealand

20. Vienna (Austria), Bratislava (Slovakia), Budapest (Hungary) and Belgrade (Serbia)

Quiz 75

1. Zone Improvement Plan. The five-digit system was introduced in the US in the early 1960s to speed up, or 'improve', the mail.

2. The North Pole

3. The Soviet cosmonaut Valentina Tereshkova in 1963.

4. Dominican Republic

5. Croydon. Croydon Airport was London's main airport in the 1930s and '40s. However, a lack of expansion room saw it close down in 1959.

6. Thailand

7. Uganda, Tanzania and Kenya

8. Iraq

9. A) A lizard. It's one of the world's few species of venomous lizard.

10. Milan. It's in the church of Santa Maria delle Grazie.

11. South Dakota

12. Angola

13. B) Roads. They can all be prefixed with the word 'Via'.

14. B) Palace of the Winds (although it is made of pink sandstone).

15. Billabong

16. C) Catholicism

17. Quito in Ecuador

18. B) An aerial shot of circular fields formed using 'center-pivot irrigation' in Kansas, USA.

19. Finland. Suomi is also the native name of the Finnish language.

20. A) UK, B) US, C) China, D) Japan, E) France, F) Germany

Quiz 76

1. *Downtown Abbey*

2. C) Kruger National Park, which was established in 1926.

3. Nepal

4. Stuttgart

5. Cumulonimbus

6. B) The glow-worms that illuminate the walls. Visitors can take boat rides beneath walls lit up by thousands of glowing beasties.

7. Iceland

8. Milk

9. Liechtenstein

10. The Beaufort Wind Scale

11. Patent office

12. C) An annual meteor shower that happens in August as the Earth passes through a cloud of debris ejected by the comet Swift-Tuttle.

13. *Catch 22* by Joseph Heller

14. B) Malawi

15. Euclid

16. The Akkadian Empire

17. Giacomo Casanova

18. Cattle testicles. Mmmm.

19. A) A bird. The turacos are a family of birds that are common in sub-Saharan Africa. They include go-away birds, so-called because of their loud warning calls.

20. Bulgaria, Croatia, Czech Republic, Denmark, Hungary, Poland, Romania and Sweden

Quiz 77

1. Colorado, Utah, Arizona and New Mexico

2. B) Diocletian

3. B) A carnivorous marsupial from Australia

4. Hokusai. It shows a wave towering over Mt Fuji. The image was the first print in a series entitled *Thirty-Six Views of Mt Fuji.*

5. A) Venice. It was the area of the city where the Jewish population was compelled to live by the authorities from 1516 onwards.

6. A) Okra

7. B) The Sundance Kid

8. C) 1994 – although the first proposal for such a tunnel was put forward in 1802.

9. Moai

10. C) Jupiter, which takes just 10 hours to spin once on its axis.

11. Clarence Birdseye. He developed the process, in which packets of fish were frozen between super-cooled metal belts, after observing the Inuit of Canada freezing freshly caught fish under thick ice.

12. B) The Inca Empire in South America. He was killed by invading Spanish conquistadors in 1533.

13. B) Hovercraft

14. A) Zambia

15. B) New Zealand

16. B) Australia, by the indigenous people of, respectively, the Torres Straits Islands, the Northern Territory, and Western Australia.

17. The Fountain of Youth (although there is no

Answers

contemporary evidence to suggest that was what he was doing, and his death in 1521 suggests he didn't find it).

18. Tanzania

19. Venezuela. It's 979 m (3211 ft) high.

20. Going west to east: Ecuador, Colombia, Brazil, São Tomé and Príncipe, Gabon, Republic of Congo, Democratic Republic of Congo, Uganda, Kenya, Somalia, Maldives, Indonesia and Kirabati

Quiz 78
Food and Drink

1. A) Spain with 1.25 million tonnes (1.4 million tons). Italy is second with 428,000 tonnes (470,000 tons) and Greece third with 346,000 tonnes (380,000 tons), according to 2018 figures.

2. C) Cured in a lime juice marinade, and then eaten raw

3. Saffron

4. Cocoa beans (or chocolate, which is where the word derives from).

5. C) Parwill. In an attempt to reclaim sales from rival spread Marmite, the makers of Vegemite changed its name so they could market it with the spectacularly awful slogan: 'Mar might but Parwill'. It proved about as successful as you'd expect and seven years later the name was changed back again.

6. C) Small flat sausages

7. On the Moon. It's the meal that Neil Armstrong and Buzz Aldrin sat down to in the lunar module during the Apollo 11 mission in 1969.

8. C) Heart, liver and lungs – collectively known as the 'pluck'.

9. Sheep's stomach

10. New Zealand

11. Fried chicken feet (the 'walkies) and heads ('talkies').

12. Apple

13. In the USA in the late 19th century, by Chinese immigrants.

14. A) A beer made from fermented maize

15. A spicy meat kebab

16. Jamaica. The seasoning has two main ingredients: Scotch bonnet peppers and allspice.

17. D) McFish 'n' Chips, England

18. B) Recooked

19. Brazil

20. A) Germany, B) Kenya, C) Thailand, D) Turkey, E) Mexico, F) Brazil, G) Denmark, H) Netherlands, I) China, J) Australia, K) Belgium, L) Canada, M) Czech Republic, N) India, O) Italy, P) Jamaica, R) Japan, S) Singapore, T) South Africa, U) Poland

Quiz 79

1. Papua New Guinea. It accounts for over 10% of all the world's languages, although most are spoken by fewer than 1000 people.

2. A) Ethiopia

3. Hamburg. It has 1.8 million inhabitants, compared with Berlin's 3.6 million.

4. Mars

5. Antarctica. They're research stations operated by, respectively, Argentina, the UK, Australia, Russia, Japan and the USA.

6. Uruguay. A giant representation of fingers reaching out of the sand, La Mano ('The Hand') is on Brava Beach in the resort of Punta del Este and is the work of the Chilean artist, Mario Irarrázabal.

7. C) So'm

8. A) Denmark. It lies in the Baltic Sea.

9. *The Grapes of Wrath* (1939) by John Steinbeck

10. Australia. It's near Shark Bay in Western Australia.

11. B) Lyon

12. Botswana

13. Hong Kong, where it's the centrepiece of the Cheung Chau Bun Festival in May.

14. B) Abraham Darby III. His grandfather, Abraham Derby I, had pioneered a new method for smelting iron.

15. C) Toronto, Canada

16. 632 CE

17. Chile, in the capital Santiago. It's better known as the Gran Torre Santiago ('Great Santiago Tower').

18. Kim Il-sung

19. A) Chamonix, France. The second, in 1928, was in St Moritz, Switzerland, while the third was held in Lake Placid, USA, in 1932.

20. A) Australian Dollar, B) Brazilian Real, C) Chinese Yuan renminbi, D) Euro, E) Great British pound sterling, F) Indian rupee, G) Norwegian krone, H) Russian ruble, I) US dollar, J) South African rand

Answers

Quiz 80

1. Chile, in the city of Algarrobo. The pool is 1,013 m (3,323 ft) long, covers an area of 8 hectares (20 acres) and contains around 250 million litres (66 million gallons) of water.

2. The Netherlands

3. B) Saskatchewan

4. C) Tehran, in Iran. It was completed in 1971 for the '2500 year celebration of the Persian Empire'. Ironically, it's believed the vast sums spent on the monument and other celebrations by the Shah (king) of Iran helped stir up the protests that led to the Iranian Revolution which ended the 2500 years of Persian monarchy.

5. C) In northeast Niger in the middle of the Sahara Desert.

6. He disappeared while swimming off a beach (in Victoria) and was declared dead – although no body was ever found.

7. A) 1920 in Antwerp

8. The Philippines. They are a range of over 1200 small, grass-covered hills that turn a chocolatey brown colour in the dry season.

9. B) Planes. The beach lies right next to an international airport and planes fly as low as 30 m (100 ft) overhead. Standing in the jet blast of a plane getting ready to take off (and risking being blown into the sea) is a popular beach activity.

10. B) Belize. It measures 318 m (1043 ft) across and is 124 m (407 ft) deep.

11. Argentina. The paintings in the Cueva de las Manos date back to between 9000–13,000 BCE and were made by the artists blowing paint through bone pipes over their outstretched hands.

12. C) Aachen Cathedral, Germany

13. Saigon

14. A) China. It's the Yancheng Dafeng Dream Maze (China) in Yancheng, Jiangsu, which opened in September 2017 and encompasses an area of 35,597 sq metres (383,160 sq ft).

15. The cane toad

16. Finland

17. Myanmar (Burma). It's said to balance on a single strand of the Buddha's hair.

18. Malta

19. Vienna

20. A) Argentina = Right
B) Australia = Left
C) Brazil = Right
D) Canada = Right
E) China = Right
F) Japan = Left
G) Kenya = Left
H) Pakistan = Left
I) Russia = Right
J) South Africa = Left
K) UK = Left
L) USA = Right

Quiz 81

1. B) Delta Airlines

2. They belong to Australia, 3830 km (2380 miles) away, but are closest to Antarctica, which is 1630 km (1010 miles) away

3. Ice hotel. It's melted and been rebuilt every year since.

4. B) 2000

5. Driver ants, which are found throughout East Africa. The jaws of the soldier ants are so large and powerful that local people sometimes use them as impromptu surgical staples, getting the ants to bite a wound closed and then snapping off the body.

6. A) Dinosaur footprints. In Cretaceous times, the rock face was a riverbed where at least eight species of dinosaurs left their marks. The mud of the riverbed hardened into rock and, over millions of years, tectonic movements gradually pushed the rock into an upright position, forming cliffs.

7. C) Canada

8. The red kangaroo

9. Roberto Baggio

10. B) Turkey. It was banned by the country's first leader Kemal Atatürk in order, as he saw it, to break with traditions and help turn Turkey into a modern state. Interestingly, the wearing of the fez had only become widespread since 1829 when the then Ottoman Sultan Mahmud II banned the wearing of turbans in a previous attempt to modernise the state.

11. Israel

12. A) Just 10, which would have left the sky mildly grazed at worst. Its revolutionary steel frame, rather than its height, paved the way for its much taller successors in the 20th century. It was torn down in 1931.

13. The giraffe

14. The Mid-Atlantic Ridge

15. Helsinki, Finland is the

Answers

most northerly Scandinavian capital at 60.17°N, followed by Oslo, Norway at 59.95°N and Stockholm, Sweden at 59.32°N. But Helsinki lies to the south of Reykjavík, which is at 64.13°N.

16. Montevideo, the capital of Uruguay, which is just slightly further south than Buenos Aires, the capital of Argentina.

17. The Pacific. They form part of French Polynesia.

18. A) The starling. The original 60 he released have since grown into a population of more than 200 million birds and are now considered a major pest. He also introduced the house sparrow, which now numbers in excess of 500 million, but that was nearly 30 years earlier in 1852.

19. C) 1912. Born in 1906, Puyi was just a child when forced to give up his imperial title, bringing to an end a role that dated all the way back to 221 BCE, when the first emperor Qin Shi Huang unified the warring Chinese states.

20. The US states are: Illinois, Indiana, Michigan, Minnesota, New York, Ohio, Pennsylvania and Wisconsin. The Canadian province is Ontario

Quiz 82
Museums

1. France. He was born Jacques-Louis Macie, but moved to England as a child where his name was anglicised to James Smithson. Exactly why he left his money to found the Smithsonian in Washington DC remains something of a mystery, as he not only never visited the city, but never set foot in the United States during his lifetime.

2. Antwerp, Belgium

3. Cape Town

4. C) Lanzarote

5. The Terracotta Army

6. Berlin

7. C) Cambridge, England

8. A) Australia. It's the Melbourne Museum.

9. C) Zagreb, Croatia

10. A) Malaysia, in Melaka City

11. Catherine the Great

12. A) British Museum, London

13. The Rijksmuseum, Amsterdam

14. The Victoria and Albert Museum

15. C) Saltar

16. B) Waxworks

17. The Ashmolean Museum

18. C) Turin

19. A) Beijing

20. It's the Guggenheim Museum in Bilbao, Spain.

Quiz 83

1. C) Grand Central Terminal, New York with 44. Shinjuku has 36, while Waterloo is a mere baby with 24.

2. Glasgow

3. The Australian pound, which was a non-decimal currency divided into shillings and pence along the lines of the British model.

4. C) Live maggots. The cheese is made with sheep's milk and then left in a place where cheese flies can lay their eggs in it. These hatch en masse (each fly can lay up to 500 eggs), with the larvae feeding on the cheese and excreting a digested form that is (apparently) extremely smooth and soft. The cheese is eaten with the (live) maggots still in it (of course).

5. Chile

6. A) *Explorer 1*. *Vanguard 1* was the second US satellite (and the fourth overall) and is the oldest human-made object still in orbit. Made by Italy in 1964, *San Marco 1* was the first satellite not built by either the US or the Soviets (although it was launched on an American rocket).

7. A) Turkey

8. Johann Sebastian Bach (1685–1750)

9. B) Chickpeas

10. B) 32 – one for each London borough.

11. Marrakesh in Morocco

12. C) Atlantic City, New Jersey, USA

13. Centre Pompidou

14. A snake, a particularly deadly one. Avoid.

15. Paraguay

16. Memphis, Tennessee

17. Albania. The country was invaded by Italy during the Second World War and became a communist state afterwards.

18. Bermuda

Answers

19. Rwanda

20. A) Bajtra is a prickly-pear flavoured liqueur from Malta, B) Crème de cassis is a blackcurrant-flavoured liqueur from France, C) Ginja is a sour-cherry-flavoured liqueur from Portugal, D) Goldschläger is a cinnamon-flavoured liqueur from Switzerland, E) Grand Marnier is an orange-flavoured liqueur from France, F) Kahlúa is a coffee-flavoured liqueur from Mexico, G) Kruškovac is a pear-flavoured liqueur from Croatia, H) Limoncello is a lemon-flavoured liqueur from Italy, I) Midori is a melon-flavoured liqueur from Japan, J) Pastis is an aniseed-flavoured liqueur from France

Quiz 84

1. Kenya

2. C) An Australian fruit, also known as a native peach or, in botanical circles, as a *Santalum acuminatum*.

3. Mumbai (formerly Bombay)

4. C) A soldier

5. French Guiana. The territory is an overseas French department – essentially a part of France in South America – and so shares its currency with the country on the European mainland.

6. B) Hippo

7. A) Paul Gauguin, either of an overdose of laudanum or a heart attack, or possibly the latter caused by the former.

8. Japan. It was the first spacecraft to reach the Moon that had not been launched by either the USA

or the Soviet Union.

9. Venice, Italy

10. C) Cubes. Strange as it may seem, wombat poop looks like brown building blocks. The animals use their faeces to help mark their territory and its unusual shape helps it to stay put on top of logs and rocks.

11. Afghanistan

12. Liberia

13. Crocodile

14. Richard Wagner

15. Simón Bolívar

16. Denmark

17. Dom Perignon – although he didn't, as is often stated, invent sparkling champagne, but he did make important contributions to its development.

18. C) Democratic Republic of Congo, which has nine neighbours (Central African Republic, South Sudan, Uganda, Rwanda, Burundi, Tanzania, Zambia, Angola and the Republic of Congo). Zambia and Tanzania both have eight each.

19. Iceland

20. Athens (1896 and 2004), Paris (1900, 1924 and the forthcoming games in 2024), London (1908, 1948 and 2012), Los Angeles (1932, 1984) and Tokyo, Japan (1964 and 2020)

Quiz 85

1. A) In the morning. As they're an unsmoked sausage that was developed in the days before refrigeration, they're supposed to be made fresh each day and eaten as soon as possible – according to tradition, before the church bells chime noon.

2. India. It was a symbol adopted by the Buddhist Emperor Ashoka who ruled nearly all of the Indian subcontinent from c. 268 BCE to 232 BCE.

3. B) Ivory Coast, in the administrative capital Yamoussoukro. When completed in 1990, it surpassed St Peter's in Rome as the largest church.

4. Argentina, Chile, Colombia and Uruguay

5. Montmartre

6. New Zealand

7. Barbados

8. A pig

9. Senegal. It's now a Unesco World Heritage Site and home to a museum and memorial dedicated to the horrors of the Atlantic slave trade.

10. Texas. It became independent when the Mexican province of Tejas broke away from Mexican control in 1836, before being annexed by the US ten years later.

11. B) Czech Republic with an average of 143 litres (31 gallons) per person. Austria is third (106 litres/23 gallons) and Germany fifth (104 litres/22 gallons), while Namibia is second with 108 litres (24 gallons).

12. The Bahamas

13. B) 80 beats per second is the record set by the amethyst woodstar hummingbird of South America.

14. A) Reims

15. C) Japan. Also known as Kinkaku-ji, it's a Zen Buddhist temple in Kyoto built in the late 14th century (and rebuilt in 1955 following an arson attack).

Answers

16. Nauru. At 21 sq km (8.1 sq miles), only Monaco and the Vatican City are smaller.
17. Aardvark
18. Greece
19. Victoria Falls
20. Russia, Finland, Sweden, Norway, Iceland, Denmark (Greenland), Canada and USA

Quiz 86
Seas and Oceans

1. C) 96.5%
2. Sargassum, a type of seaweed that grows there in abundance.
3. Challenger Deep. It lies 10,916 m (35,814 ft) beneath the surface.
4. The fin whale. It can grow up to 25.9 m (85 ft) long and weigh up to 74 tonnes (82 tons).
5. The Southern Ocean
6. The Red Sea and the Mediterranean Sea
7. Turkey. The Black Sea and Aegean Sea (part of the Mediterranean Sea).
8. The Coral Sea
9. The Bermuda Triangle, an area of the Atlantic Ocean where it's claimed various ships and planes have mysteriously disappeared.
10. C) 70%
11. The Aral Sea
12. The sperm whale, which can grow up to 20.5 m (67 ft).
13. B) 1.6 million sq km (600,000 sq miles) or roughly three times the size of France.
14. The Gulf Stream
15. B) An undersea volcanic island that doesn't reach the water's surface
16. Bioluminescence
17. Plankton floats, nekton

swims, while benthos inhabits the sea floor.
18. The Deepwater Horizon
19. The sea otter, which has an incredible 140,000 hairs per square cm (almost a million per square inch). By way of comparison, an average dog has around 2100 per square cm (15,000 per square inch), while we humans have a rather feeble 140 hairs per square cm (1000 per square inch) on the top of our heads. Without the blubber of other marine animals, the otter relies on its thick pelt to keep warm.
20. B) Abyssal Plain

Quiz 87

1. B) 55,000. Spread out over an area of 2.16 million sq km (836,000 sq miles), that amounts to just 0.03 people per sq km (0.1 per sq m).
2. Lake Baikal, Russia
3. 1896
4. C) A small antelope
5. Colombia. *Bollo* is a type of bun made from yuca, corn or potatoes.
6. Occidental
7. Gandhi
8. Montreal. Botswana.
9. Uruguay
10. Peter Carey
11. A) Italy
12. Bangladesh
13. A) Egyptian pound
14. Andorra. Under its constitution, the ceremonial heads of state are whoever is currently the head of state of France and the Bishop of the Catalan town of La Seu d'Urgell.

However, it is the prime minister who retains the country's executive power.
15. North Carolina
16. Nikita Khrushchev
17. South America
18. B) Tattooing – using a thin chisel called an *uhi*.
19. A) Pyongyang, the capital of North Korea. The tall triangular building is the 105-storey Ryungyong Hotel, begun in 1987 and still unfinished.
20. Panama, Costa Rica, Nicaragua, Honduras, El Salvador, Guatemala and Belize

Quiz 88

1. C) The Netherlands
2. The Mekong
3. The International Space Station. The planet Venus is fourth.
4. Regent's Park
5. Buenos Aires
6. The quokka
7. C) Lisbon. In Portuguese, it's known as Padrão dos Descobrimentos.
8. C) Mexico, in Tijuana, where he was working to avoid the restrictions of Prohibition then in force in the USA.
9. Guano, or bird droppings, which in the 19th century was mined in huge volumes for use as a soil fertiliser.
10. Africa. It's an island off its west coast.
11. Nepal. It consists of two triangle shapes, one above the other.
12. B) Ethiopia
13. A) Alluvial gold nugget (gold that's been eroded away from

Answers

a main lode by the action of water). It weighed 109.59 kg (293.5 lb) and measured 61 by 31 cm (24 by 12 in). There's a commemorative obelisk marking the find site. The nugget was melted down into ingots, but there's a replica in Melbourne's City Museum.

14. Cleopatra's Needle – although neither obelisk has any connection with the Egyptian queen, both being over a 1000 years old when she came to the throne.

15. C) South Carolina, the first state to secede from the Union. It was readmitted after the war in 1868.

16. C) Ithaca

17. The five landing beaches used during the Second World War D-Day Normandy landings of 1944.

18. Colombia

19. A) *SS Great Eastern*. It measured 211 m (692 ft) and was intended to be a passenger liner capable of carrying 4000 passengers from England to Australia without refuelling. However, it wasn't a great success and was used instead as a cable-laying ship and, later, as a floating music hall.

20. *Provinces*: Ontario, Québec, Nova Scotia, New Brunswick, Manitoba, British Columbia, Prince Edward Island, Saskatchewan, Alberta, Newfoundland and Labrador. *Territories*: Northwest Territories, Yukon and Nunavut

Quiz 89

1. B) Sheep

2. The Ganges. The glacier is located in the Indian portion of the Himalayas.

3. Diamonds. Kimberlite pipes are rocks in which diamonds have formed at great pressure deep in the Earth's crust, and are occasionally brought to the surface by volcanic eruptions.

4. A) Kiribati, then Samoa, then Tonga, which all lie just west of the International Date Line.

5. B) Gunpowder. The target is designed to explode (in a small way) when hit.

6. *Mary Rose*. The ship is now displayed at a purpose-built museum in Portsmouth.

7. Russia. Dug between 1970 and 1989, it was originally supposed to reach a depth of 15,000 m (50,000 ft), but was abandoned when the drill broke.

8. Nova Scotia

9. The contiguous United States... just. The USA is 4313 km (2680 miles) wide while Australia is 4041 km (2511 miles) wide.

10. The Bronx

11. C) Dwarf planet

12. Thailand

13. The Amazon

14. B) Syria

15. A) The pangolin, or spiny anteater, which lives in Africa and Asia, where it is much in demand for both its meat and its scales, which some people believe have medicinal properties.

16. France, Switzerland, Austria and Slovenia

17. A) Vanuatu

18. Tunisia. The ruins of Carthage lie near the city of Tunis.

19. A) 1904

20. The river rises in Germany and then, from west to east, passes through or alongside Austria, Slovakia, Hungary, Croatia, Serbia, Romania, Bulgaria, Moldova and Ukraine, before emptying into the Black Sea.

Quiz 90
Space

1. B) A German V2 rocket. This flying bomb, the first guided ballistic missile, was designed by the German Wernher von Braun who, following a secret move to the US after the war, would go on to act as the chief architect of the rocket programme that put the first men on the Moon.

2. Proxima Centauri. 4.22 years.

3. The far side of the Moon. Earth's gravity has locked the Moon's rotation so it always shows the same face to Earth. This marked the first time the other side had been seen.

4. India. It stands for the Indian Space Research Organisation.

5. A) Salyut 1. It was launched by the Soviets in 1971.

6. B) It's the site of Russia's main space launch facility – although it's technically located in Kazakhstan and is leased to the Russians. The Baikonur Cosmodrome has been the launch site of most of the major Soviet and Russian space missions.

7. Pluto

8. C) 99.8%

Answers

9. A) *Sojourner* in 1997, followed by *Opportunity* (and its twin *Spirit*) in 2003, and *Curiosity* in 2012.

10. C) It doesn't travel at all. Sound is made of vibrations travelling through air (or another medium, such as water) and, as space is an almost perfect vacuum, it means the *Alien* movie poster is true: 'In space, no one can hear you scream'.

11. Manned Maneuvering Unit

12. 1981. Columbia.

13. Big Bang. Ironically, Hoyle didn't accept the theory and used the term dismissively to contrast it with his own 'steady state' theory of the universe.

14. The Sun. SOHO stands for 'Solar and Heliospheric Observatory'.

15. The Asteroid Belt. They are both large asteroids.

16. C) 2003. He travelled aboard the *Shenzhou 5* spacecraft.

17. B) *Voyager 2*. Launched in 1977, it has visited all four of the gas and ice giants in the outer solar system: Jupiter in 1979, Saturn in 1981, Uranus in 1986 and Neptune in 1989.

18. Sally Ride in 1983

19. The International Space Station. The work of five space agencies – American, Russian, Japanese, European and Canadian – the ISS was constructed between 1998 and 2011 at a cost of $160 billion.

20. A) Pluto, B) Neptune, C) Uranus, D) Saturn, E) Jupiter

Quiz 91

1. Hollywoodland. It was originally just an advert for local real estate and nothing to do with the film industry.

2. Buenos Aires

3. Reykjavík, Iceland

4. The Eureka Rebellion

5. C) Rome. The volcano was Mt Vesuvius.

6. Marrakesh. The name comes from the red sandstone used for many of its buildings.

7. Frank Gehry

8. Delhi

9. Osborne House

10. The Atacama Desert in northern Chile

11. Thomas Jefferson

12. Addis Ababa. More than 40,000 people take part.

13. Ice. In the days before mechanical refrigeration, ice was exported around the world for cold storage. Wenham ice was regarded as particularly pure, especially so in Britain where there was huge demand for it – so much so that ice from other sources was often passed off as Wenham ice.

14. South Africa. It's on its southwest coast between Mossel Bay and the Storms River.

15. Sailing. It's a race for sailing yachts staged between international sailing clubs.

16. Venice

17. Denmark

18. Panama and Colombia. It's known as the Darién Gap.

19. Berlin. The island's collections include the Altes Museum, the Neues Museum, the Alte Nationalgalerie, the Bode Museum and the Pergamon Museum.

20. A) Emmental = Switzerland, B) Cotija = Mexico, C) Marscapone = Italy, D) Gouda = the Netherlands, E) Feta = Greece, F) Domiati = Egypt, G) Manchego = Spain, H) Halloumi = Cyprus, I) Stilton = England, J) Paneer = India, K) Roquefort = France, L) Adelost = Sweden

Quiz 92

1. Denmark. Hot dogs are a popular street food bought at a *pølsevogn* ('sausage wagon'), and often accompanied by chocolate milk.

2. Comets. It's thought that many long-period comets – those that take over 200 years to orbit the Sun – come from this region.

3. Swahili. It means 'journey'.

4. Pennsylvania

5. Pennsylvania

6. B) It's mainland Europe's westernmost spot

7. Melbourne. However, owing to strict quarantine laws, the horse-riding events were held on the other side of the world in Sweden.

8. C) Ethiopia. It's located in Addis Ababa.

9. Alaska. It spilled 41 million litres (10.8 million gallons) of oil.

10. Jerusalem

11. The Severn

12. The Northwest Territories

13. Varanasi

14. Auckland, New Zealand

15. *Rosetta*. It orbited comet 67P/Churyumov–Gerasimenko,

Answers

releasing a lander called *Philae* onto its surface, although it failed to attach properly.

16. South Africa

17. A) Ushuaia, Argentina

18. A human pyramid

19. The First Transcontinental Railroad across the USA

20. Algeria, Angola, Ecuador, Equatorial Guinea, Gabon, Iran, Iraq, Kuwait, Libya, Nigeria, Qatar, Republic of Congo, Saudi Arabia, United Arab Emirates and Venezuela

Quiz 93

1. C) 1905

2. A river dolphin

3. C) Nothing – except the location of the storm. Certain terms tend to be used in certain places, but using another one isn't technically incorrect. So the term 'hurricane' is generally used in the North Atlantic, central North Pacific and eastern North Pacific; the term 'typhoon' is generally used in the Northwest Pacific; and the term 'cyclone' is generally used in the South Pacific and Indian oceans.

4. C) Bungee jumping. In summer, men from the island jump from tall wooden towers, up to 30 m (100 ft) high with vines tied to their feet, a practice they believe will ensure a good yam harvest.

5. Antarctica. He made the discovery aboard the ship *Vostok*. One hundred and forty one years later, Yuri Gagarin would become the first human to set eyes on space in a spacecraft named in its honour, *Vostok 1*.

6. B) Frankfurt

7. The Federal Reserve System, which is headquartered in Washington DC.

8. The People's Bank of China, which has headquarters in both Beijing and Shanghai.

9. Indonesia

10. New Orleans

11. A sandwich, made with a baguette and filled with meats and pickled vegetables.

12. Sardinia

13. B) Sweden. Built at a scale of 1:20 million, the Sun is represented by the Ericsson Globe in Stockholm, an indoor arena with a diameter of 110 m (361 ft). The models of the planets are not just the correct relative sizes, but also the correct relative distances, which means that the model of the furthest planet, Neptune, measures 2.5 m (8.2 ft) across and is set 229 km (142 miles) from the Globe in the coastal town of Söderhamn.

14. The coconut crab

15. Cartagena, Colombia

16. Prague, Czech Republic

17. Niagara Falls

18. It was awarded to the winners of the FIFA World Cup. When Brazil won the tournament for a third time in 1970, it was allowed to keep the trophy (named after the FIFA president who founded the World Cup) and a new trophy was commissioned for the 1974 World Cup.

19. B) The Pantheon Rome. Built by the emperor Hadrian in around 126 CE, this former temple (now a church) is one

of the best-preserved of all Roman buildings.

20. France, Switzerland, USA, Germany, Norway, Italy, Austria, Japan, Yugoslavia, Canada, Russia, South Korea. The USA has hosted it the most number of times: four.

Quiz 94
Changing Places

1. Bonn

2. Tanganyika and Zanzibar

3. Truth or Consequences, which was the name of the show. The show's producers had organised a competition, promising to broadcast the tenth anniversary programme from whichever town changed its name to match the show. Hot Springs took up the challenge. It's now more commonly referred to as 'T or C'.

4. Islamabad was the newly built capital, while Rawalpindi served as the interim capital.

5. Zaire

6. Canberra, which replaced Melbourne as capital of Australia.

7. Oslo

8. Ankara

9. Rio de Janeiro

10. Rhodesia (or Southern Rhodesia)

11. New Delhi

12. Kyoto

13. St Petersburg

14. The Seychelles

15. Iran

16. Cambodia

17. Ghana

18. Thailand

19. British Honduras

20. Jakarta

Answers

Quiz 95

1. New Mexico
2. Their names mean, tautologically, 'Hill Hill'. Pen means 'hill' in Cumbric, a medieval language once spoken in the north of England, Bryn means 'hill' in Welsh and Berge means 'hill' in Norwegian.
3. Bangkok (most locals refer to it as Krungthep, which is a little easier than the full version).
4. B) Australia. It runs between Brisbane and Cairns.
5. Burkina Faso
6. A) Ham. The two-year old chimp flew for just over 16 minutes in space, performing some basic tasks, such as lever pulling, before splashing down successfully in the Atlantic Ocean, where he was recovered. He lived until 1983.
7. A) Hong Kong
8. C) Central Park, which opened in 1858, and was largely based on Birkenhead Park in Liverpool, England, which had opened a decade earlier.
9. Guyana
10. Morocco
11. C) The Tube map. He based it on an electrical circuit diagram, emphasising how lines interconnect rather than representing the actual distances between the stations.
12. C) Located in Connecticut, it's not a lake at all, but the United States' oldest continuously operating amusement park.
13. A) Malaysia. It's the Sarawak chamber.
14. B) 476. The year 410 marked the end of Roman rule in Britain, while 1453 saw the final collapse of the Eastern Roman Empire when Constantinople fell to the Ottoman forces.
15. A) Armenia
16. New Zealand
17. A rubber tree
18. Tanzania
19. Pol Pot
20. The Netherlands

Quiz 96

1. Las Vegas
2. C) Namibia, with an estimated 3500 animals.
3. Bolivia
4. New Zealand
5. *Ulysses* by James Joyce. All the events described in the book take place in Dublin on a single day, 16 June 1904.
6. Grenada
7. A) Observatory
8. B) A live duck in a basket. *Pato* means 'duck' in Spanish.
9. C) Babies, specifically babies born in the previous 12 months. The ritual is supposed to ward off illness and evil spirits.
10. A stamp. The 1847 Mauritian blue and red penny stamps are among the rarest in the world. Those in the museum's collection were bought for $2 million in 1993.
11. C) Wang
12. The Kelpies – kelpies are shape-shifting water spirits from Scottish myths. The statues are the work of the Scottish artist Andy Scott.
13. Korean
14. Flamingo
15. Being the first (and last)

captain of the *Titanic*.
16. B) Below your feet. It marks the boundary between the solid rock of the Earth's crust and the molten rock of the mantle. It's named after the Croatian seismologist Andrija Mohorovičić.
17. Zambia
18. Mallorca
19. Italy
20. United Nations Educational, Scientific and Cultural Organisation

Quiz 97
US State Capitals

1. B) Montgomery
2. B) Juneau
3. C) Sacramento
4. B) Denver
5. C) Hartford
6. B) Tallahassee
7. A) Atlanta
8. B) Springfield
9. B) Des Moines
10. A) Topeka
11. A) Frankfort
12. A) Baton Rouge
13. A) Boston
14. B) Carson City
15. C) Lansing
16. A) St Paul
17. B) Santa Fe
18. C) Albany
19. A) Raleigh
20. A) Columbus
21. A) Salem
22. B) Harrisburg
23. A) Austin
24. C) Salt Lake City
25. B) Olympia

Answers

Quiz 98

1. Hawaii. They were named in honour of the then head of the Royal Navy, the Earl of Sandwich, rather than the comestible.
2. C) Double Gloucester
3. Bolivia. It's situated near Lake Titicaca.
4. C) The most abundant wild bird is believed to be the red-billed quelea, with a population of around 1.5 billion birds in sub-Saharan Africa.
5. A) Australia
6. Wales. Welsh is still spoken by some of the people there, although it is no longer the language of the majority.
7. C) Reims
8. West African CFA Franc. CFA stands for Communauté Financière Afrique ('Financial Community of Africa').
9. Marco Polo. *Il Milione* ('The Million') is usually known as *The Travels of Marco Polo* in English.
10. Brahma ('the creator')
11. Lake Malawi
12. Jerusalem
13. Manaus
14. C) Nottingham
15. C) Marigold
16. B) Tasmania
17. Ecuador, in Quito
18. B) 95
19. St Louis
20. UK, France, Spain, Algeria, Mali, Burkina Faso, Togo and Ghana

Quiz 99

1. A) Bristlecone pine
2. Turin (1861–65). Florence (1865–70).
3. C) Saiga. The eland and nyala are African antelopes.
4. Avignon
5. Vietnam
6. B) Cabo Verde, where it is considered the national music
7. Saturn. Its landing on Titan was the furthest landing from Earth yet made by a spacecraft.
8. Brisbane
9. C) Just 0.04%
10. The Festival of Britain, which was held exactly 100 years after the Great Exhibition.
11. Québec City
12. B) Shanghai
13. Paris. It's the Grande Arche de la Défense in the city's business district, which was completed in 1989.
14. Chuck Yeager. The American pilot broke the barrier in an experimental plane, *Bell X-1*, in 1947, hitting a speed of 1,235 kph (767 mph).
15. C) A bird
16. Mozambique
17. The Philippines
18. Tokyo
19. C) Shrimp. The first Portuguese explorers named the coast Rio dos Camarões, after noting the large numbers of the crustaceans living there.
20. Bosnia and Hercegovina, Croatia, Republic of Macedonia, Montenegro, Serbia, Slovenia and Kosovo

Quiz 100

1. St Vincent and the Grenadines (not Jamaica; that's Kingston).
2. Dogs (not birds – the birds were named after the islands). The name comes from the Latin *canariae insulae*, meaning 'island of dogs'.
3. The Antonine Wall, which was a stone and turf fortification built around 160 km (100 miles) north of Hadrian's Wall. It was ordered by the Roman Emperor Antoninus Pius, who never visited Britain (unlike Hadrian). The wall was abandoned around 50 years after it was begun.
4. Mohandas. Mahatma was a title meaning 'venerable' bestowed on him in his forties.
5. Victor Verster. He spent most of his time in jail in Robben Island prison, but had been transferred here by the time he was released in 1990.
6. New York. It's a memorial in Central Park near the Dakota building where John Lennon lived – and where he was killed in 1980. The Liverpool Children's Home which inspired the song is actually called Strawberry Field.
7. A) 1 – Russia, which has borders with both.
8. Spanish flu, not the First World War. In fact, the devastating flu, which lasted from 1918 to 1920, proved deadly among all sections of society right across the world, killing an estimated 100 million people, or around 4% of the then global population.
9. Sudan, not Egypt. While there are an estimated 120 pyramids in Egypt, there are around 220

Answers

in Sudan, where the Nubian civilisations of Kerma, Napata and Meroe flourished alongside the Nile at much the same time as (and often interacting with) the Egyptians, from around 2600 BCE to 330 CE.

10. Northwest (check it on a map if you don't believe it).

11. Glasgow. Although the film is set in Edinburgh, it was actually filmed almost entirely in Glasgow.

12. Eight: Noah himself along with his wife and their three sons (Shem, Ham and Japheth) plus their three wives. None of the wives' names are mentioned in the Bible.

13. C) 116 years, from 1337 to 1453. The war was actually a series of conflicts between England and France over French territorial possessions.

14. B) France. The company was founded by an Italian, Ettore Bugatti, in 1908, but the company has always been based in the town of Molsheim, which was once in Germany, and is now part of France.

15. C) Chimborazo, in Ecuador. Although *just* 6,263 m-high (20,549 ft), it lies very close to the Equator where the Earth bulges, meaning it lies further from the core than the other two.

16. November, by modern calculations. At that time, Russia was still using the old Julian calendar. It didn't switch to the Gregorian calendar being used by most of the rest of the world until after the revolution.

17. Lego. According to the latest available figures, Lego produces over 300 million tyres a year, compared with under 200 million by its main rivals, Bridgestone and Michelin. Obviously, the tyres are a lot smaller.

18. Bright orange – to make it easier to spot in a crash site. 'Black box' is just a colloquialism.

19. Paul von Hindenberg. Hitler was appointed chancellor early in 1933, and later appointed himself Führer but was never officially president of Germany.

20. 12. The number never changes, regardless of how many countries are currently in the Union.

Published in 2019 by Lonely Planet Global Limited
CRN 554153
www.lonelyplanet.com
ISBN 978 1 78868 123 0
© Lonely Planet 2019
Printed in China
10 9 8 7 6 5 4 3 2 1

Managing Director, Publishing Piers Pickard
Associate Publisher Robin Barton
Writer and Editor Joe Fullman
Art Direction & Design Dan Di Paolo
Print production Nigel Longuet

Picture Credits
Key: p= page, t=top, b=bottom, l=left, r=right, c=centre
Getty Images: p8 SeanPavonePhoto; **NASA:** p116; **Shutterstock.com:** p13 Tono Balaguer,
p16 aphotostory, p17 Dietmar Rauscher, p19 Iakov Filimonov, p21 Marco Rubino, p24 Ricky Edwards,
p25 photravel_ru=, p26 canadastock, p28 Aeronautics, p32 Artgraphixel, p33 coopermoisse,
p34 Dan Rata, p35 irisphoto1, p36 tl cl br Ray_of_Light, bl lts design, tr Yoko Design, cr chuckstock,
p37 tl cl Ray_of_Light, bl lts design, tr Sugiyarto, cr br Yurkalmmortal, p40 Ron Ellis, p52 f11photo,
p54 Nuaehnaja, p57 David Bostock, p58 Cezary Wojtkowski, p61 Vichy Deal, p64 tbate54, p69 Zhao
jian kang, p74 meunierd, p78 Ilona Ignatova, p79 tl kyslynskahal, p79 cr CCat82, p80 mbrand85,
p81 Gabriele Maltinti, p83 Skycolors, p88 Vaclav Sebek, p89 chrisdorney, p90 Albert Russ,
p114 Aerostato, p115 DestinationsInNewZealand, p120 elbud, p123 Manuel Ascanio, p125 Trinacria
Photo, p126 Pierpaolo Romano, p128 artistVMG, p134 Pavel Ilyukhin, p135 Luckies, p137 DebsG,
p138 Fredrikande, p139 cl Gang Liu, p139 cr photo.ua, p141 Xtuv Photography, p142 Ecuadorpostales.

STAY IN TOUCH
lonelyplanet.com/contact

AUSTRALIA
The Malt Store, Level 3, 551 Swanston St, Carlton, Victoria 3053, **T:** 03 8379 8000

IRELAND
Digital Depot, The Digital Hub, Roe Lane, Dublin 8 D08 TCV4

USA
124 Linden St, Oakland, CA 94607, **T:** 510 250 6400

UK
240 Blackfriars Rd, London SE1 8NW, **T:** 020 3771 5100

Paper in this book is certified against the Forest Stewardship Council™ standards. FSC™ promotes environmentally responsible, socially beneficial and economically viable management of the world's forests.